10 Things You Should Know About

God and life

GREG LAURIE

This *Billy Graham Library Selection* is published by
the Billy Graham Evangelistic Association
with permission from FM Management.

A *Billy Graham Library Selection* designates materials that are appropriate for a well-rounded collection of quality Christian literature, including both classic and contemporary reading and reference materials.

Published by the Billy Graham Evangelistic Association with permission from FM Management, Ltd., 2008.

10 Things You Should Know About God & Life
©2006 by Greg Laurie.

ISBN: 978-1-59328-210-3

Previous ISBN: 0-9777103-3-5

Printed in United States of America

Cover design: Christopher Laurie

Interior design & Production: Highgate Cross+Cathey, Ltd.

Coordination: FM Management, Ltd.

Contents

BILLY GRAHAM
Evangelistic Association

Always Good News.

Dear Friend,

I am pleased to send you this copy of *10 Things You Should Know About God and Life* by my good friend and BGEA board member Greg Laurie.

10 Things You Should Know About God and Life is a practical collection of Greg's 10 most-requested messages. Applying powerful truths from the Word of God, Greg teaches on such things as overcoming temptation, relying on God's perfect timing, and discerning His will. I pray that this book will help you—or someone you know—grasp the victorious life that God desires for each of His children.

For nearly 60 years the Billy Graham Evangelistic Association has worked to take the Good News of Jesus Christ throughout the world by every effective means available, and I'm excited about what God will do in the years ahead. If you would like to know more about our ministry, please contact us:

In the U.S.:

Billy Graham Evangelistic Association
1 Billy Graham Parkway
Charlotte, NC 28201-0001
billygraham.org
webmaster@billygraham.org
Toll-free: 1-877-2GRAHAM (1-877-247-2426)

In Canada:

Billy Graham Evangelistic Association of Canada
20 Hopewell Way NE
Calgary, Alberta T3J 5H5
billygraham.ca
Toll-free: 1-888-393-0003

We would appreciate knowing how our ministry has touched your life. May God bless you.

Sincerely,

Franklin Graham
President

Introduction

Every year it's pretty much the same. When we roll into December, we are barraged by all the lists of what stood out, or was notable in the previous twelve months. What were the top ten news stories of the past year? What were the top ten songs or movies or resort destinations or rides at Disneyland?

Sometimes we're even treated to the "bottom ten" worst ones!

The lists just go on and on. What you hold in your hands is a top ten list of my own. This book contains the top ten messages I have given over the last year. Let me explain. I didn't choose these topics, our radio listeners did. Every day our radio broadcast, *A New Beginning*, is heard around the world. These broadcasts are essentially edited versions of messages I have preached at the church I pastor here in Riverside, California: Harvest Christian Fellowship.

So, over the last twelve months, these particular messages are the ones those listeners chose as their favorites. These are the topics that resonated most with them, the ones they responded to above the others.

I could have come up with a list of *my* favorites, but that really wouldn't make much sense. I'm not preaching for me. So as I was putting together this book, I thought I would go with what the people thought—people from around the globe. Frankly, I was surprised by some of the ones they chose...*pleasantly* surprised. And even though these topics seem to cover the gamut—from knowing God's will to parenting—from wrestling with temptation to divorce-proofing your marriage—the messages really do speak to the critical issues of our lives.

In short, the chapters that follow are about God and life.

Hence the title.

Hence the book.

I trust and pray that these messages will also resonate with you, as they have for so many others.

God bless you,
Greg Laurie
June 13, 2006
Riverside, California

What is a Christian?

I heard the story of a man who had been down on his luck, and was desperate to make a little money. After a few other doors had closed to him, he had the idea of going to the city zoo, hoping to land a job feeding the animals. The manager at the zoo had no openings, but seeing how big this guy was, he offered him another possible position.

"Say, our gorilla died the other day, and he was one of our most popular exhibits. If we got you a special gorilla suit, would you put it on and imitate him for a few days, until the new gorilla arrives? We'll pay you well for it!"

Well, when you need a job you need a job. The man was so desperate for work he agreed. In fact, after a few hours, he really got into the part—beating his chest and shaking the bars. Huge crowds were gathering. *Maybe this won't be so bad after all, he told himself.*

The money was pretty good, he could take naps in the sunshine, he had all the bananas he could eat, and really, when he thought about it, there were a lot worse jobs. But one day, right in the middle of his gorilla act, he was swinging on a trapeze and lost his grip. What was worse, his momentum carried him right over a tall chain link fence into the middle of the lion's den. Looking up at this intruder in his domain, the huge lion gave a ferocious roar. The crowds were mesmerized, really getting into this jungle drama.

But what was a gorilla to do? He realized that if he cried out for help, it would reveal his true identity.

He slowly walked backwards away from the lion, hoping to climb the fence back into his own cage. The lion, however, with a hungry look on his face, began to stalk him step by step. Finally, in desperation, the gorilla hollered, "Help!"

Immediately the lion answered in an annoyed whisper, "Shut up, stupid! You'll get us both fired!"

You see…things aren't always as they appear!

And there are many people today who claim

to be Christians—who may even *think* they are Christians—but are not.

A QUICK LOOK AT THE NUMBERS

Just how "Christian" is our nation these days? As I studied the matter recently, I was a little surprised by the statistics I encountered.

In a magazine article entitled, "What Does America Believe?" researchers revealed the following: 86 percent of Americans polled believed in God or a Supreme Being, while 75 percent expressed a belief in an afterlife. A surprising 86 percent expressed belief in a heaven, while 77 percent believed in a hell. Over half the respondents did not believe that humans evolved from lower life forms.

These numbers would seem to show that we are a nation of believers—at least in something. But the same poll showed that 10 percent believed Elvis was still alive!

Another news magazine did their own survey. The pollsters found that 60 percent of Americans say they attend religious services regularly, and only about 9 percent profess no religion at all. More than 80 percent—including 71 percent of college graduates—believe the Bible is the inspired Word of God. Of that number, 34 percent believe the Bible should be taken as literal, word-for-word truth.

What's more, those percentages seem to be on the rise, rather than falling, as you might expect. Another pollster asked respondents whether they agreed or disagreed with the statement: "Prayer is an important part of my daily life." The number of people who responded positively to that statement in the statistics I had before me rose from 41 percent to 53 percent over a ten-year period—an amazing surge of 12 percentage points.

Those who asserted that they never doubted the existence of God rose 11 points in that same ten-year period. Even more amazing, 46 percent of Americans who responded to the survey described themselves as "born again."

A highly publicized study released by the graduate school of City University in New York found that 7 out of 8 Americans identify with a Christian denomination. So much for "secular America"! Apparently, even as political correctness seeks to ban all expressions of Christian faith in public places, America is outgrowing its old "take it or leave it" attitude toward religion. Now even people without faith are "looking for God"—or at least would describe themselves as being into some kind of "spirituality."

But how much do they really understand?

A Barna study done among teenagers related that 86 percent claim that they are Christian. At the same time, however, Christian teenagers are rapidly distancing themselves from the truths of the Bible. Teens are more likely than adults to reject the existence of Satan, to believe in salvation by good deeds, and to reject the idea that Jesus was sinless. Only one-third described themselves as "absolutely committed" to Christianity, half say they are moderately committed, and the remaining one-fifth are even less committed.

Back to some of the polling data I quoted earlier: Of those who said they read the Bible regularly, the respondents admitted they were "uncertain about its features." For example, half of them couldn't name even one of the four gospels of the New Testament; the other half could name at least one. Fewer than half knew who delivered the Sermon on the Mount. Sixty percent of Americans attended church last Easter, but one-fourth didn't know what the occasion signifies!

WHAT DOES BEING A CHRISTIAN REALLY MEAN?

I'm reminded of a group of four-year-olds being questioned by their teacher in a Sunday school class. Looking across at those bright little faces, the teacher asked this question: "Does anyone know what today is?"

A little girl held up her hand and said, "Yes, today is Palm Sunday."

"That's fantastic!" the teacher said. "That's wonderful. Now, does anyone know what *next* Sunday is?"

The same little girl lifted her hand. "Yes," she said, "next Sunday is Easter Sunday."

The teacher was all smiles. "Oh, *very* good. Now…does anyone know what makes next Sunday Easter?" On a roll, the same little girl responded, "Yes, next Sunday is Easter because Jesus rose from the grave." Before the impressed teacher could congratulate her, however, the girl added, "but if He sees His shadow, He has to go back in for seven weeks."

It's clear that many people really don't have a grasp on what it means to be a believer. Do you? Are you one? Are you sure? What exactly is a Christian? Are you born that way? If not, how exactly do you become one? What are the requirements?

In 2 Corinthians 13:5, Paul wrote: "Examine yourselves to see if your faith is really genuine. Test yourselves. If you cannot tell that Jesus Christ is among you, it means you have failed the test."

Check up on yourselves, Paul was saying. Are you actually believers? Do you pass the test? Or are you just pretending to be (or hoping to be) a Christian when actually you aren't at all?

How can we tell if someone is really a Christian? More importantly how can you be sure if *you* are one? Jesus said, "Therefore by their fruits you will know them" (Matthew 7:20). So let's do a little "fruit inspection," and look together at some clear biblical principles about what must happen as a result of someone truly finding Jesus Christ as his or her personal Lord and Savior.

When you ask someone if he or she is Christian, one of the most common responses you get back is, "Of course I'm a Christian. I go to church, don't I?" That's like saying I am a golfer because I own a set of golf clubs. Or I'm a surfer because I own a pair of board shorts. Listen, to be a golfer you need to golf, to be a surfer you must surf, and to be a Christian means you need to walk with God!

Going to church doesn't make you a Christian any more than going to a doughnut shop makes you a cop!

DON'T ALL ROADS LEAD TO GOD?

Now you might say, "Why is it so important that I be a Christian, anyway? Don't all roads basically lead to God?"

Not according to Jesus!

Jesus said, "Most assuredly, I say to you, unless one is born again, he cannot see the kingdom of God" (John 3:3). Only Jesus Christ—and no other—died on the cross for your sins. Only He promises you the hope of heaven. And no other religion teaches that! Jesus essentially said the only way you can be certain your sins are forgiven and to know you will spend eternity in heaven is by putting your complete trust in Him. And there will be tangible results to show you have done that.

Now don't misunderstand me, I am not suggesting that "X" amount of good works makes you a Christian. Far from it. In fact, all the "good works" on earth will not save you.

The Bible says, "He saved us, not because

of the good things we did, but because of his mercy. He washed away our sins and gave us a new life through the Holy Spirit" (Titus 3:5).

This, in fact, is one of the main things that sets Christianity apart from all other world religions. All other religious systems essentially say "Do!" "*Do* this and you will have 'good karma,' or you will get to heaven, or paradise, or nirvana...." In contrast, Jesus Christ says, "Done!" That's what it meant when He cried out on the cross, saying, "It is finished!"

The transaction is complete.
The price has been paid.

But please understand this: If we have discovered that the price has been paid, if we believe, and if we receive His payment for our sins, it will mean radical changes taking place in our lives! Have those changes taken place in your life yet? If you were arrested for being a Christian today, would there be enough "evidence" to convict you?

The Bible says, "Therefore, if anyone is in Christ, he is a new creation; old things have passed away; behold, all things have become new"

(2 Corinthians 5:17). Honestly, does that describe your life?

If you were to ask "man on the street" what one must do to be a Christian, he would probably say: "Believe that Jesus is the Son of God. Believe in miracles, heaven, and hell. Go to church, pray, read the Bible, and keep the Ten Commandments. And—oh yeah—probably be baptized. And start living a good life."

Right now I am going to make a statement that may be shocking to you: *You can do all those things I just mentioned and not necessarily be a Christian!* Don't get me wrong; if you are a true Christian you *should* do all of those things. But the outward change is often without the inward, but the inward change is never without the outward.

IT'S WHAT'S INSIDE THAT COUNTS

Let's take a closer look at some of the elements of this "outward-inward" phenomenon.

#1: A person may pray and still not really be a Christian.

In fact, if we're to believe the statistics, 9 out of 10 people in our nation pray. Recent scientific studies have verified the fact that prayer—even when the afflicted person has no knowledge of

it—improves the health of those who are sick.
In addition to this, 76 percent believe God is a
heavenly Father who can be reached by prayers.

But that doesn't necessarily mean you are truly
a believer! Most of us pray when we're in trouble or
the "chips are down." What's the first thing on the
lips of most people when they are confronted by a
crisis? You've heard it. "Oh my God!" It's a prayer
whether they admit it or not.

But when the storm passes, when the crisis
blows over, what then?

In the book of Jonah all the pagan sailors called
on their successive gods when the awesome storm
at sea threatened their lives. It was true of me, too,
before I was a Christian. Whenever I found myself
in a tight spot, I called out to God.

People also pray to appease their guilt-ridden
conscience. It may be more accurate to say they
"offer prayers," instead of truly praying. Jesus told
of a self-righteous Pharisee at prayer in the temple,
who "stood and prayed thus with himself" (Luke
18:11). God said of Israel, "These people draw
near with their mouths and honor Me with their
lips, but have removed their hearts far from Me"
(Isaiah 29:13).

You may pray with all the passion and regularity in the world, but if you have not admitted to God that you are a sinner, and lost without Him, if you have not sought His forgiveness and salvation through the Lord Jesus Christ, it won't do you any good. The psalmist wrote: "If I regard iniquity in my heart, the Lord will not hear me" (Psalm 66:18, KJV).

#2: A person may make some visible changes in life, and yet still not be a Christian.

The book of Acts tells a fascinating story about a man named Simon, who got caught up in the excitement of an evangelistic crusade in Samaria:

A man named Simon had been a sorcerer there for many years, claiming to be someone great. The Samaritan people, from the least to the greatest, often spoke of him as "the Great One—the Power of God." He was very influential because of the magic he performed. But now the people believed Philip's message of Good News concerning the Kingdom of God and the name of Jesus Christ. As a result, many men and women were baptized. Then Simon himself believed and was baptized. He began following Philip

wherever he went, and he was amazed
by the great miracles and signs Philip
performed. (Acts 8:9–13, NLT)

That must have been big news in town. It
probably made the headlines of the *Samaritan
Times.*

Simon the Sorcerer Baptized!

Apparently leaving his life of occultism and
witchcraft, he claimed belief in Christ, and even
took the step of baptism. The truth is, Simon had
operated a neat little religious racket for years.
And there's something about the title of "The
Great One—the Power of God" that goes to your
head just a little. It became obvious that he didn't
want to let go of that prestige. But in view of the
evangelistic crusade rocking the city, he realized he
needed to make some quick changes. He needed to
"get religion."

It's no different today. People will "get
converted" to get what they want. A non-Christian
guy asks an attractive and virtuous Christian girl
out on a date. But she turns him down, saying,
"Sorry, I only date Christians."

Then, suddenly, the nonbeliever is saying,
"Oh…praise God! I'm really into this Christian

thing, too." Probably not! And it will only be a matter of time before the mask falls off and his true motives are revealed.

That's how it turned out for Simon-the-reformed-sorcerer.

> Then Peter and John laid their hands upon these believers, and they received the Holy Spirit. When Simon saw that the Holy Spirit was given when the apostles placed their hands upon people's heads, he offered money to buy this power. "Let me have this power, too," he exclaimed, "so that when I lay my hands on people, they will receive the Holy Spirit!"

> But Peter replied, "May your money perish with you for thinking God's gift can be bought! You can have no part in this, for your heart is not right before God. Turn from your wickedness and pray to the Lord. Perhaps he will forgive your evil thoughts, for I can see that you are full of bitterness and held captive by sin."

> "Pray to the Lord for me," Simon exclaimed, "that these terrible things won't happen to

me!" (Acts 8:17–24, NLT)

When Simon's true motives were suddenly revealed, he came face to face with himself and the darkness of his own heart. I like to think that he turned to the Lord in earnest at that point...but the Bible doesn't say.

In another example, the Bible tells us of King Herod, who had a great respect for John the Baptist, found himself strangely drawn to the message, and even made some changes in his life as a direct result of John's influence. Yet because of the pressure of others (primarily his wicked wife, Herodias) he had John beheaded—and his heart grew hard as stone (Matthew 14:1–10).

#3: You can live a good life, be religious and even to the best of your ability keep the Ten Commandments and still not necessarily be a Christian.

Think for a moment of the account of the rich young ruler in the gospels. One of the accounts tells us that, in his eagerness, he came running up to Jesus. Breathless, he said, "Good Teacher, what good thing shall I do that I may have eternal life?"

Jesus told him, "If you want to enter into life, keep the commandments." And then the Lord told him which ones.

The young man said to Him, "All these things I have kept from my youth. What do I still lack?" (See Matthew 19:16–20.)

Look how far this earnest young man had gone: He not only heard the commands of God, he kept them. To the best of his ability he kept all of them. And not only that, but he had done it since childhood!

But he didn't go far enough! *He stopped short of Jesus.*

The story concludes with the young man turning his back on the Lord and walking away sadly. And there is no record that he ever came back to Jesus.

It just goes to show that contact with holy things, if they do not convert and change the heart, can actually harden the heart. If the listener sees the light of Jesus Christ, and then turns away from Him, he or she is plunged deeper into darkness.

Knowledge brings responsibility! And my friend, you can no longer claim ignorance after you read this chapter!

There are a number of examples in the pages of the Bible of people who came close to God… close to Jesus…but stopped short. They were so

near, and yet so far. We think first of Judas, who
perhaps more than any other man in Scripture was
absolutely without excuse! He was the "hypocrite
extraordinaire," fooling everyone but Jesus.
Think of it. He personally heard the Sermon on
the Mount, witnessed the miracle feeding of the
multitudes, and was an eyewitness when Lazarus
was raised from the dead. And in the end, he came
close enough to Jesus to actually kiss Him…as he
was betraying Him to death.

So let's summarize. The outward without
the inward is only an empty shell. You can pray,
believe in miracles, and still not necessarily be
a Christian. You can hear the Gospel and even
believe in its truth, and still not be a Christian. You
can live an exemplary life, be religious, and keep
the commandments of God from earliest memory
and still not be a Christian. You can be in church
with other believers, hear the same message,
receive communion, and even believe that Jesus is
coming back, and still not be a Christian. And like
Simon, you can appear to be a believer and even be
baptized and still not be a Christian.

WHO THEN IS A CHRISTIAN?

The problem with all the people I have cited in this chapter, Simon, King Herod, the rich young ruler, and Judas, is that true conversion did not precede their "Christian activity." While it is true, as the apostle James tells us, that faith without works is dead, it could also be said that works without faith are also dead.

So what steps must be taken to know one is truly a Christian? The real question before us is one that man has been asking for years. The Philippian jailer put it so clearly when he cried out, *"What must I do to be saved?"*

Paul's response was significant, "Believe on the Lord Jesus Christ and you shall be saved" (Acts 16:31).

Fine…but what does "believing" actually *mean*? The Bible says that even the demons from hell believe, and tremble at what they know very well to be true (Acts 2:19). Here are the essential elements of the Good News that we must believe and receive to become a born-again child of God.

THE ESSENTIAL ELEMENTS OF BELIEF

#1: Realize that you are a sinner.

This is a hard pill for some people to swallow, but it is an essential fact. Romans 3:23 tells us that

"All have sinned and fallen short of the glory of God." In other words, sin has infiltrated the human race and not one of us has escaped its effects.

The Bible tells us that this sentence of death goes all the way back to Adam, the first man, who with his wife, Eve, ate forbidden fruit in the garden. Sin entered the human race through Adam, and the human race has been trying without success to live above it, restrain it, civilize it, or get rid of it ever since. The history of the human race from that day in the Garden to this has been man's futile effort to gain back the position lost by Adam's fall.

We might protest and say, "Why should I be held responsible for what some guy named Adam did thousands of years ago?"

Look at it this way....Adam acted as the head of the human race, even as the President of the United States is the head of the government. When the president acts, it is really the American people acting through him. When the president makes a decision (whether we like it or not, agree with it or not), that decision stands as the decision of the entire people. In the same way, Adam acted on our behalf.

But don't be too quick to jump down Adam's throat.

If we had been in his position, we would have done the same thing. In fact, every day of our lives we face the same test that was set before Adam. We are confronted with hundreds and even thousands of decisions to do the right or wrong thing. And let's be honest here…so often we choose the wrong.

God says, "I have set before you life and death, blessing and cursing; therefore choose life, that both you and your descendants may live" (Deuteronomy 30:19).

The Bible says that prior to coming to faith, we are dead in our trespasses and sins. The word used here for "sins" is *harmatia*—"to miss the mark." It was a term used in archery. This phrase came to represent missing or falling short of any goal, standard, or purpose.

No human being in his or her own strength has hit that mark: not Billy Graham, not Mother Teresa, not my godly mentor Chuck Smith, and certainly not Greg Laurie. Some of us may miss the bull's eye farther than others, but not one of us has hit it.

Why? Because God's "mark" is *absolute, total, complete, flawless perfection!* Jesus said, "Be perfect even as your Father in heaven is perfect."

To miss the mark would certainly include what we might call the sin of omission—the things you ought to have done but didn't do.

A Sunday school teacher once asked her class, "Who can tell me the difference between the sins of *commission and omission*?" A girl in the back row said, "A sin of commission is doing what is wrong."

"Very good," the teacher replied. "Now who can tell me what the sin of *omission* is?"

A little boy was waving his hand back and forth until the teacher finally called on him, "The sin of omission," he said, "are those sins you want to do but haven't gotten around to yet!"

#2: Repent of your sins.

"Repent"? That's certainly a word that we don't hear very often today. But the fact of the matter is, it is the first recorded word to have fallen from the lips of Jesus after He began His ministry. *"Repent for the kingdom of heaven is at hand" (Matthew 3:2).* The Bible says, "God has commanded men everywhere to repent." Jesus said, "Unless you repent, you too will all perish" (Luke 13:5, NIV).

So obviously "repent" is a pivotal word. But

what does it mean?

It means to "change" or to "turn." It's like driving down the highway, pulling a U-turn, and heading the other direction. More than simply being sorry, it is a word of action. Many people feel remorse for their sin but never truly repent. Remorse is being sorry, repentance is being sorry enough to stop.

Paul wrote: "God can use sorrow in our lives to help us turn away from sin and seek salvation. We will never regret that kind of sorrow. But sorrow without repentance is the kind that results in death" (2 Corinthians 7:10, NLT).

In the story of the prodigal son, the young man knew he was wrong—probably knew it from the beginning. But nothing changed until he acted on that knowledge, crawled out of the pig pen, and started down the road toward his father and home. He had a "change of mind" that resulted in a "change of direction."

#3: Believe in and receive Jesus Christ into your life.

Repenting is turning away from one thing, while faith is turning to another.

In salvation, you are turning from sin to Jesus Christ.

From darkness to light.

From the power of Satan to the power of God.

And it is a choice only you can make.

The Bible says, "But as many as received Him [Jesus], to them He gave the right to become children of God, to those who believe in His name" (John 1:12).

Jesus said, "For God so loved the world that whosoever believes in Him should not perish" (John 3:16).

This is because you realize that Jesus Christ is the very Son of God. He is the One who loves you so much that He died on a cross for you 2,000 years ago to pay the penalty for your sin, and then rose from the dead three days later. You need to believe that, and ask Him into your life.

#4: Do it NOW!

Good intentions are not enough. Agreeing with what I have said in this chapter is not enough. You must admit you are a sinner, repent of that sin, and put your faith in Christ. The prodigal son could have repeated that refrain, "I am no longer worthy…" over and over again. He could have said it the rest of his life, and remained in the far country, separated from his father and home. But he did more than repeat those words. He acted on them. He got up and started walking. You must do the same.

When?

The Bible says, "Now is the day of salvation."

As with the prodigal, that first step might be a difficult one to make. But how glad he was when he felt his father's arms around him, and heard the words, "Welcome home."

Handling Difficult
Questions

Most of us can remember the encounter all too clearly.

We felt moved in our hearts to offer a word of eternal hope to a friend, a family member, or a co-worker. As carefully and lovingly as we knew how, we began to share the Good News of salvation in Jesus Christ with that individual. And suddenly we found ourselves absolutely barraged with a string of attacks, difficult arguments, and questions.

How do we respond? Either we will determine to never confront anyone ever again with the Gospel (which would be disobedience), or we can seek to follow the command of Scripture and get ourselves ready to answer some of those questions that come up again and again. Remember the apostle Peter's words?

Always be prepared to give an answer to

everyone who asks you to give the reason
for the hope you have. But do this with
gentleness and respect, keeping a clear
conscience, so that those who speak
maliciously against your good behavior in
Christ may be ashamed of their slander.
(1 Peter 3:15–16, NIV)

The word Peter uses for *answer* in this passage
comes from the Greek word *apologia*. That word
may sound like *apology*, but don't get the wrong
idea! We have nothing to apologize for when we
share the Good News of sins forgiven and eternal
life in Christ. Actually, *apologia* means to present
a verbal defense to everyone who asks you for a
logical explanation.

Be ready, says Peter, with a verbal defense of
the Gospel.

There are people out there—more than we
begin to realize—who truly do have honest
questions. Maybe it's just one thing—one hang
up—that Satan has used as a barrier in their mind
for years. And when you give them a good answer,
it's as though you "rolled away the stone" for them
to come out of their tomb of unbelief.

Of course, that's not the way it is with everyone.

With some people, as soon as you answer their first question, they've got five more to pull out of the hat. *But why this? What about that? How could…? What if…? Do you mean…? Are you saying that…?* They have all the reasons lined up why they can't come to Christ before you even finish dealing with the first one.

May I let you in on a little secret here? *These people don't really want your answers.* What they want to do is get you flustered and off track.

As communicators of the Gospel, we need to stay calm, gracious, and on track as we speak the truth in love. Jesus, the Master Communicator, modeled this so well for us. In John 4, the Samaritan woman at the well in Sychar tried to sidetrack Him again and again with one hot-button issue after another. But Jesus returned to the most important thing of all in that moment: her eternal soul.

That's the way it often is when you seek to tell someone about your faith in Christ. They want to distract you, discourage you, and bury you with all manner of objections. These so-called "reasons" are often nothing but a smokescreen for the *real* reason. For there is one primary reason (or excuse) for people refusing to come to Jesus for salvation.

That reason may surprise you.

I'll identify it for you after we deal with four of the "big questions" people often ask when you seek to tell them about Christ.

THE FOUR BIG QUESTIONS

#1: If God is so good and loving, why does He allow evil?

Sound familiar? This one almost always tops the list. You've heard it in a score of versions. *Why does He allow babies to be born blind? Why does He allow wars to rage, killing innocent people? How could He stand by and let a little girl be kidnapped, raped, and murdered? What about all the horrible injustice in the world? How could He allow this terrible tragedy…this hurricane… this tsunami…this earthquake…this wildfire… this epidemic…to take place when He could have prevented it?*

In the classic statement of the problem, either God is all powerful but not all good, therefore He *doesn't* stop evil…or He is all good but not all powerful, therefore He *can't* stop evil. The general tendency, of course, is to blame God for evil and suffering, and pass all responsibility on to Him.

Let's go back to that question a moment: *If God is so good and loving, why does He allow evil?*

First of all, this question is based on a false premise. If I make such a statement, I am essentially suggesting (or saying outright) that God is not "all good." And why am I saying that? Because He doesn't meet my criteria of being good and allowing evil at the same time.

So often the person you're talking to imagines that they are the first one to ever come up with this question. And in their minds, it's so airtight and irrefutable that it puts a period on the whole issue right there.

But it really doesn't. Not at all.

The first question I would ask in response would be, *"So when did you become the moral center of the universe?"* Listen, God is not good because I think He is good, or because I personally agree with what He says and does. God is good because He says He is! Jesus said, "No one is good, except God alone" (Luke 18:19). God is good if I believe it or not. He and He alone is the final court of arbitration. As Paul said, "Let God be true, and every man a liar" (Romans 3:4, NIV).

What is "good"? *Good is what God approves.*

We may ask, "Why is what God approves good?" Answer: Because He approves it! That is to say, there is no higher standard of goodness than God's own character, and His approval of whatever is consistent with that character.

So God is good. Period.

Now let's come back to the second part of the question. *Why does He allow evil?*

We must remember man was not created evil, but perfect. Ageless. Innocent. Immortal. From the very beginning, however, from the time God breathed the breath of life into that inanimate clay, man has had the ability to choose right or wrong.

And he made his choice.

Had man never sinned, there would have been no resulting curse. Romans 5:12 (NLT) tells us: "When Adam sinned, sin entered the entire human race. Adam's sin brought death, so death spread to everyone, for everyone sinned."

The point we must keep in mind is that man, not God, is responsible for sin. But why didn't God make man so he *couldn't* sin?

Because that would make us less than man, created in His image. Part of that image of God within us is a free will—a capacity to choose good or evil, to do right or wrong. It sometimes seems that it would be a much better (and certainly safer) world if God did not allow us to exercise our free will.

Free will is our greatest blessing and in many ways our worst curse. If God hadn't given us free will, we would merely be marionettes on a string, remote control robots that bow before Him at the touch of a button. God, however, wants to be loved and obeyed by creatures who voluntarily choose to do so. Love is not genuine if there is no other option.

After the September 11, 2001 attack on the World Trade Center and Pentagon, I was asked one question again and again. *"Why did God allow this?"* Some even said, "This was obviously the judgment of God."

I don't agree with that.

Jesus spoke about a "current news story" of His own day, in Luke 13:4–5. A tower had apparently collapsed in Jerusalem, crushing a group of eighteen men. Referring to that local headline, He asked the rhetorical question, "Were they the worst sinners in Jerusalem? No, I tell you again that unless you repent, you will also perish."

Did these people fall under some special, targeted justice of God? Did they get their comeuppance because they were all notorious rebels and God-haters, and judgment fell?

No, Jesus was saying. The bottom line is, people die.

And here was His point: *"You'd better be careful, because you might die, too! You too are a sinner, and this could happen to you as well. Those people weren't any worse or better than you!"*

Tragedies happen. Wars happen. Accidents happen. Illness happens. Cancer happens. We live in a broken, fallen world, and nobody's exempt. It could happen to me. I could get hit by a car or die in a plane crash or succumb to a heart attack—or have a tower fall on me. One out of one people on earth die! Enoch and Elijah may have dodged that final bullet, but besides these two, there are no exceptions. Lazarus may have been raised from the dead, but in a few years, he had to die all over again.

This doesn't mean that God is unfair. It doesn't mean He has singled out me or anybody else for special judgment. If I die, it just means that it was my time to leave this earth. And that time will come to *everybody*.

The Bible says, "It is appointed unto men once to die…" (Hebrews 9:27, KJV). One meaning of that word *appointed* in the original language is "reserved."

You've got an advance reservation for when you will leave this world for an eternal destination. There's a ticket with your name on it and the time of your departure. That's not a gloomy, pessimistic view of life if you belong to Jesus Christ. If you're a Christian, that whole concept of inevitable death is flooded with hope! You know that when you pass from this life, you will step immediately into the majesty and radiance of the Lord's immediate presence, and live with Him forever. What's not to like about that?

Paul told his friends in Philippi, "For to me, to live is Christ, and to die is gain…. Yet what I shall choose I cannot tell. For I am hard-pressed between the two, having a desire to depart and be with Christ, which is far better" (Philippians 1:21, 22–23).

You would never hear that imprisoned apostle saying, "Well, if I've got to die, then I've got to die. Not much I can do about it anyway." No, to

Paul, dying meant coming out ahead in the game! Stepping out of this life into the next was the best thing he could imagine. Being in the presence of the Lord Jesus wasn't just "better," it was "*far better.*"

The simple truth is, tragedies have wracked this planet since Adam and Eve were pushed out of the Garden of Eden, and they will continue until Jesus Christ returns to earth to set up His rule of righteousness. But God in His mercy can also take the tragedies of life and *use* them—for our good and for His eternal glory. Nothing is wasted! Not one sigh, not one tear, not one groan in our spirit.

You remember the story of Joseph. His wicked brothers betrayed him and sold him into slavery. But in what could have been the ultimate moment of payback, Joseph instead said, *"But as for you, you meant evil against me; but God meant it for good, in order to bring it about as it is this day, to save many people alive"* (Genesis 50:20).

That means that God can take the most evil deed and work *in spite* of it. And even work *through* it and *in* it. Romans 8:28 tells us, "And we know that all things work together for good to those who love God, to those who are the called according to His purpose." This includes what we perceive as "good things" as well as "bad things."

It's hard for us to understand how a bad thing could ultimately work for the good of anyone. In themselves, there's certainly nothing "good" about illness, car crashes, war casualties, or terrorist attacks. But God in His infinite wisdom and love somehow takes all the events of our lives—both good and bad—and *blends* them together ultimately for our good, the good He intends for our lives.

When I was a young boy I lived with my grandparents. "Mama Stella" made the best buttermilk biscuits I have ever tasted—and she would do it every night! (That was living!) There were many times when I would stand there in the kitchen and watch her making those heavenly creations from scratch.

With her incredible skill, she knew just how to prepare them. As I look back on that time, however, I have to admit that there isn't even one single ingredient in those biscuits I would have enjoyed by itself.

Buttermilk? Ecch!

Cooking oil? Of course not.

Self-rising flour? How would I even eat it?

But these elements were carefully mixed together by Mama Stella's expert hands, and then placed in a very hot oven for just the right amount of time. When they were done they were—in my opinion—the closest thing to manna from heaven!

The "all things" of Romans 8:28 are like the ingredients of biscuit dough. By themselves they're not tasteful to us. We shun them. And we certainly shun the heat of the oven! But when God in His infinite skill has blended them all together and cooked them properly in the oven of adversity, we will look back one day and say, "It was good."

Please don't misunderstand me. Not all that happens is good. Evil is still evil, heartbreak is still heartbreak, and grief is still grief. There are many things in the course of our lives that are very hard to bear. Even so, all things *work together* for good. As Christians, we cling to the hope of Revelation 21:4:

> And God will wipe away every tear from their eyes; there shall be no more death, nor sorrow, nor crying. There shall be no more pain, for the former things have passed away.

Now, that doesn't mean I can always explain why certain tragedies happen. I can't. I'm as outraged as anyone by injustices; trials and traumas can shake me, too. But when I come to something I don't understand, I try to fall back on what I *do* understand. It's one of those instances of "it's not what you know, it's who you know." And I know the One who has the answer to every question. Not so very long from now, I'll be able to ask Him anything I've ever wanted to know. But I have a feeling that once I'm drinking in my first view of the Son of God in all His glory and wonder, many of the issues that so troubled me on earth suddenly won't seem very important.

#2: How can you Christians say, "Jesus is the only way"?

"Are you saying Jesus Christ is the ONLY way, and that if someone doesn't believe in Him, they're actually going to hell? That's so narrow! So insensitive! So intolerant!"

By insisting that Jesus is the only way to approach God, I may sound to certain people like I'm implying I'm somehow better than they are. Or that I look down on them in some way.

But I have a very good reason for believing that Jesus Christ is the only way to the Father, and it has nothing to do with my cleverness or wisdom. I believe it because He *said* so. It isn't my theory, it isn't my idea, it is His! It was Jesus who clearly stated, "I am the way, the truth, and the life. No one comes to the Father except through Me" (John 14:6).

How plain is that?

What part of "NO ONE" don't we understand?

And the bottom line is either we're going to believe everything Jesus said, or nothing that He said. As for me, I choose to put my faith and trust in Him—for my years here on earth, and for my eternity.

In Acts 4:12, the apostle Peter declared, "Nor is there salvation in any other, for there is no other name under heaven given among men by which we must be saved."

Paul told Timothy, "For there is only one God and one Mediator who can reconcile God and people. He is the man Christ Jesus" (1 Timothy 2:5, NLT). If I claim to be His follower and believe His words, then I would be less than honest if I said anything *but* this. As a Christian I am in no way better or superior to anyone else. I'm just one beggar telling another beggar where to find bread.

Maybe you've had someone say to you, "Well, all religions basically say and teach the same thing. They're all true. And besides, if a person is *really sincere* in what they believe, they'll get to heaven."

This type of fuzzy, illogical, politically correct thinking is typical of so many today—making the most important decisions of life on the basis of your feelings and opinions. That's no way to run a universe!

Let's take this line of reasoning to its logical conclusion. If a person truly is sincere in what they believe, and tries to live a good life, then they will get to heaven. So Adolf Hitler is in heaven, right? He sincerely believed what he was doing was right. He had a sincere view of racial supremacy, and thought it was "right" to exterminate the Jewish people.

At this writing, I don't know if Osama Bin Laden is dead or alive. But let's say we got him and he's dead. Where do you think he is right now, heaven or hell? Most would say "hell!" But why? He was sincere in thinking Allah wanted him to kill three thousand people. He was honest and genuine about his belief that every American man, woman, and child are infidels deserving death. So…why wouldn't he end up in some kind of paradise?

"No!" you protest. "He is *not* good!"

Really? According to whose definition? Yours? Mine? The person next door? Is it determined by consensus? *Why* is it wrong to lie, steal, and murder?

This is why "sincerity" is never enough. We have to have a set of absolutes we live by. We can't simply make up the rules as we go along. You may *want* to believe that "all roads lead to God." You may really and sincerely hope that every religion is basically true, and that they somehow all blend beautifully together.

But they don't. For instance…

#1: Concerning the existence of a personal God: Buddhists deny it altogether. Hindus believe that God is formless and abstract, taking the form of a trinity as well as *millions of lesser gods*. In direct contrast, the Bible teaches that God is a personal deity, who created man in His own image, loves us, and wants to have a relationship with us.

#2: Concerning salvation: Buddhists believe salvation comes by self effort alone—with no personal God to help or guide you. Hindus believe you achieve salvation by devotion, works, and self

control. Moslems insist that man earns his own salvation, pays for his own sins, and that you can never be certain if you have achieved it or not.

In contrast, the Bible teaches that Jesus Christ died for our sins, and if we will turn from our own way and follow Him, we can be forgiven and have the hope of heaven.

#3: *Concerning Jesus Christ:* Buddhists believe Jesus was a good teacher, but less important than Buddha. Hindus believe Jesus was just one of many incarnations, or sons of God. They teach that Christ was not the one-and-only Son of God. He was no more Divine than any other man, and He did not die for man's sins. Moslems will tell you that Jesus Christ was only a man, a prophet equal to Adam, Noah, or Abraham, all of whom are below Mohammed in importance. The Koran, the Moslem scriptures, teaches that Christ did not die for man's sin. In fact, Judas, not Jesus, died on the cross.

Do you see my point? It doesn't work to believe in "all of the above." The tenets of these religions directly contradict one another. They cannot "all be true." Buddhists, Moslems, and Hindus have no assurance that they will get to heaven.

Only Christianity holds to that wonderful, life-transforming hope.

These belief systems are diverse and contradictory. They have little to nothing in common. Jesus told the people of His day, "For if you do not believe that I am, you will die in your sins....He that is not with me is against me" (John 8:24, Luke 11:23). Jesus claimed to be the only way to the Father. It is not enough to admire Him, or to think of Him as a "great moral teacher." We must examine His unique claims and make a decision.

C. S. Lewis, the author of the "Chronicles of Narnia," and a great Christian thinker, said, "A man who was merely a man and said the sort of things Jesus said would not be a 'great moral teacher.' He would either be a lunatic—on a level with the man who says he is a poached egg—or else he would be the Devil of Hell. You can shut Him up for a fool, you can spit at Him and kill Him as a demon; or you can fall at His feet and call Him Lord and God. But let us not come with any patronizing nonsense about His being a great human teacher. He has not left that open to us. He did not intend to."

#3: How can a God of love send people to hell?

In fact, God doesn't send anyone to hell. We send ourselves there. Hell was never created for man.

> "Depart from me you cursed into the
> everlasting fire prepared for the devil and
> his angels." (Matthew 25:41)

God doesn't want anyone to go there! In the book of Ezekiel He says, "I have no pleasure in the death of the wicked...turn back from your evil ways" (33:11). Peter tells us that "God is not willing that any should perish..." (2 Peter 3:9).

There will be no one "accidentally" in hell. Nor will there be anyone "accidentally" in heaven. People will be in heaven because of a deliberate choice, and people will be in hell for the same reason.

In the same way, you do not "accidentally" become a Christian. It's the result of the choice you make. Imagine you are headed up a freeway off-ramp marked, "DANGER! DO NOT ENTER!" Police are waving to you frantically, but still you persist in driving the wrong way. If you die, who is at fault?

That is why God sent Jesus: He says, "Stop! Turn around! Why will you die in your sins?

Put your faith in Me and find forgiveness and everlasting life." But if we reject His offer, "How shall we escape if we neglect so great a salvation?" (Hebrews 2:3).

#4: What about the person who has never heard the Gospel?

God will judge us according to the "light we have received." We will not be held accountable for what we do not know. That, however, does not excuse us from all responsibility, otherwise we might say, "Ignorance is bliss."

We as humans, no matter where we live on God's earth, were born with "eternity in our hearts" (Ecclesiastes 3:11). We were born with a soul, an inner emptiness, a sense that life *should* have meaning and purpose. (And where did *that* idea come from?) In spite of an internal compass pointing toward God, we have gone our own way.

The book of Romans tells us:

> But God shows his anger from heaven against all sinful, wicked people who push the truth away from themselves. For the truth about God is known to them instinctively. God has put this knowledge in their hearts. From the time the world was created, people have seen the earth and sky

and all that God made. They can clearly see
his invisible qualities—his eternal power
and divine nature. So they have no excuse
whatsoever for not knowing God.
(Romans 1:18–20, NLT)

So we have turned against what little we know
to be true. Some would say, "Well, I have my own
standards that I live by, and they're basically good."
But if we are brutally honest with ourselves, we
would have to admit that we don't even live up to
our own standards. We continually violate even
what we admit to be true. Again, in the book of
Romans, Paul writes: "He will punish sin wherever
it is found. He will punish the heathen when they
sin, even though they never had God's written
laws, for down in their hearts they know right from
wrong. God's laws are written within them; their
own conscience accuses them" (2:12, NLT).

If a person is a true seeker of God, the Lord will
reveal Himself to them. There is a man in the Bible
known as Cornelius. Although a Roman Centurion,
he was a very religious man who prayed and sought
God with all his heart. He knew very little, if
anything, about Jesus Christ, but had been asking
God to reveal Himself to him.

God answered the prayer of Cornelius, and sent the apostle Peter to preach the Gospel to him. When Cornelius heard that wonderful message he believed—and brought everyone in his household along with him! That's because he was a "true seeker." And God promises, "You will seek Me and find Me, when you search for Me with all your heart. I will be found by you" (Jeremiah 29:13–14).

Quite honestly, the person who often asks this "What-about-those-who-never-heard" question isn't as much concerned about the stone-age tribe up some forgotten tributary of the Amazon, as they are about throwing up a "smoke screen" to keep you at a distance. He or she doesn't want to hear about personal responsibility before a holy God, and feels compelled to lock your mental gears with a question.

How then do we respond? We might remind them that God is loving and compassionate, and will deal with the person who has never heard the Gospel fairly and justly. But the issue of the moment is what will *you*—the person I'm speaking to right now—do with the truth of the Gospel? Knowledge brings responsibility, and people will be held accountable before God for what they know.

THE REAL REASON PEOPLE REFUSE TO BELIEVE

The Bible says, "And this is the condemnation, that the light has come into the world, and men loved darkness rather than light, because their deeds were evil. For everyone practicing evil hates the light and does not come to the light, lest his deeds should be exposed. But he who does the truth comes to the light, that his deeds may be clearly seen, that they have been done in God" (John 3:19–21).

"Men loved darkness rather than light, because their deeds were evil." The stark reality of this verse leads men and women to the worst sin they could possibly commit. No, it's not murder, adultery, or stealing.

It is the sin of unbelief.

If a person really wanted answers to the questions I've mentioned in this chapter, they would seek those answers out. But so many never do…and it's not because of unanswered questions. These are often nothing more than the shallow and empty excuses they hide behind. They feel a security there behind those insincere "objections" to the faith. It's comfortable. Non-threatening. It's home to them just like a pigsty is home to a pig.

They really don't want to come to the light. It's even interesting to see how many people prefer the night over the day.

Not me. I love Daylight Savings Time and the extra hour of Southern California sunlight that gives me.

But not everyone feels that way. The story is told of a castle-like prison in Paris known as the Bastille that was about to be destroyed in 1789. A prisoner who had been kept confined in a dark, dingy dungeon in this prison for many years was brought out and released. But instead of welcoming his new freedom he begged to be taken back in. It had been such a long time since he had seen the sunshine that his eyes could not endure its brightness. His only desire was to return to the darkness and die in the murky dungeon where he had been a captive.

In the same way, some men continue to reject Jesus Christ until they eventually become so hardened in their sin that they prefer the dark ways of eternal death. As Solomon wrote: "A man who remains stiff-necked after many rebukes will suddenly be destroyed—without remedy" (Proverbs 29:1, NIV).

For those, however, with a heart's desire to
tell others about the great Good News of rescue
from a life of sin and a new relationship with the
living God, there's no need to worry about who
will accept or who will reject. Yes, it is good "to
be ready always" with thoughtful, well-reasoned
answers to commonly asked questions. But most
of all, the thing God asks us to explain is the hope
and joy and peace that radiates from our hearts and
lives.

We can simply, kindly, and graciously tell the
story of what God has done for us. And there isn't
an argument in the world that can refute that.

When God
Seems Late

Has it ever seemed like God has let you down?
That He failed to come through for you
in your hour of need?

That He somehow forgot about you—or that He
was simply too late?

If you've ever felt this way you're in good
company. Some of God's most choice servants have
felt the same way.

One of the reasons for this, of course, is that
we all live on schedules. We govern our lives by
the clock…and we expect God to synchronize His
watch with ours. ("What time do You have, Lord?
I've got five minutes after the hour.")

After all…you check in at work and leave at a
certain time. You eat your meals at a certain time.
You go to class or keep your appointments at a
certain time. You even live out the years of your life
for a certain amount of time. And far, far too often,

we spend those precious hours of our lives on time-consuming non-essentials. Here's what I mean. In a lifetime, the average American will spend…

> …*six months sitting at traffic lights waiting for them to change*
> …*one year searching through desk clutter looking for misplaced objects*
> …*eight months opening junk mail*
> …*two years trying to call people who aren't in or whose line is busy*
> …*five years waiting in lines*
> …*three years in meetings*
> …*countless hours learning how to operate 20,000 different things, from pop machines to can openers to digital radio controls.*

In addition, the average American will…

> …*commute forty-five minutes every day*
> …*receive 600 advertising messages every day (including television, newspapers, magazines, radio, billboards)*
> …*watch 1,700 hours of television every year*
> …*open 600 pieces of mail every year.*

That, my friend, is a lot of wasted time! God,

of course, is not bound by our time zones, time limitations, and time restrictions. He lives above all of that, in Eternity. He has His own schedule, and He is never late. (Don't you hate it when people are?) He is always right on time. Scripture tells us, "He has made everything beautiful in its time" (Ecclesiastes 3:11).

THE LONG, LONG WAIT

Some 2,000 years ago, many in the nation of Israel probably felt as though God had lost track of time. When would the long-promised Messiah finally arrive on the scene? Was God even aware of their suffering? These were very dark and difficult days in Israel's history, rivaling the days of their bondage in Egypt under Pharaoh.

But this time, it wasn't Egypt. It was Rome. The descendants of Abraham, Isaac, and Jacob lived under the absolute tyranny of the Caesars. And if that wasn't bad enough, Caesar had set up a puppet king in Jerusalem named Herod. This man, of course, was a mockery of a king, "ruling" under the heel of Rome and murdering members of his own family in fits of jealous paranoia. It was a well-known saying that it was "better to be one of

Herod's pigs than his family."

The pigs, at least, had a chance of surviving for a few years.

To make matters worse, the people of Israel hadn't heard a word from God in *four hundred years*. No prophets. No miracles. No visions. No angelic visitations. From the time Malachi wrapped up his last prophecy centuries before, heaven had gone completely silent.

People then, of course, weren't really much different from people today. They had spiritual hunger and longed for purpose in life just as we do. Sadly, however, if they turned their spiritual searching to the Judaism of the day, they would come away empty-handed. Instead of a vibrant, living faith as in the glory days of David, Solomon, Jehoshaphat, and Hezekiah, they found an empty shell. Judaism had become a grim maze and minefield of rituals, rules, and regulations that even the religious leaders couldn't keep, much less the people on the street.

But surely…something must be on the horizon.

The coming of Messiah must be nearer than ever. Hadn't the Lord told their final prophet, "But to you who fear My name the Sun of Righteousness shall arise with healing in His wings" (Malachi 4:2)?

Arise, O Lord! How long…?

But even in these spiritually impoverished times, there were those who walked with God. There were the spiritually perceptive men and women who believed in God and rested in His promises. We read of Simeon, an old man who was "just and devout, waiting for the Consolation of Israel, and the Holy Spirit was upon him" (Luke 2:25). Simeon who waited in the temple day and night lest he miss the Messiah's arrival (and his persistence was rewarded!).

There was something in the air. An anticipation. An expectancy. To those who walked with God and sought His face, it seemed like the time was just right for God to send forth His Son.

And finally…the silence was broken. God sent Gabriel, a high-ranking angel, to announce to the godly Zechariah and Elizabeth that they would give birth to the forerunner of the Messiah.

A forerunner? Yes, and the Holy Spirit filled Zechariah's mouth with wisdom and joy when he prophesied over his newborn boy, "And thou, child, shalt be called the prophet of the Highest: for thou shalt go before the face of the Lord to prepare his ways" (Luke 1:76, KJV).

As Paul would affirm years later, "When the fullness of the time had come, God sent forth His Son, born of a woman, born under the law, to redeem those who were under the law, that we might receive the adoption as sons" (Galatians 4:4–5).

God is always on time.

He is never too early or too late.

The Messiah did indeed come, on the heels of His forerunner, John the Baptist. And those who had "eyes to see" believed on Him and put their trust in Him.

But even while the Messiah walked this earth as the prophets foretold...there was still that troubling question of God's timing. Let's look at a story that shows how even when God seems to miss His appointment or lose track of time, it all works into His perfect plan for our lives. This is a story that *shows God is never late, and that He is always right on time—His time.*

SOME LOGICAL ASSUMPTIONS

In John chapter 11 there's a moving story that's recorded by John alone.

It's the account of a family devastated by an unexpected tragedy. They were a tight-knit family, and one that happened to be very close to Jesus. I am speaking of Mary, Martha, and their brother, Lazarus.

Jesus frequented this home. He felt comfortable, loved, and appreciated there. In that home, Jesus was more than a curiosity or celebrity or controversial rabbi. He was their personal friend.

By the way, does He feel at home like that in your house? Is He comfortable there? Does He feel honored, loved, and appreciated under your roof? Paul prayed for the believers in Ephesus, "that Christ will be more and more at home in your hearts as you trust in him" (Ephesians 3:17). When Jesus walked through that doorway in Bethany, He knew that He would be welcomed with open arms. Martha would bustle around trying to serve His favorite meals. Mary would sit at His feet and soak up His every word. And Lazarus shared a deep bond of love with the Teacher.

What does Jesus encounter when He walks through the front door of your life? Does He feel like His presence is a welcome, joyous thing…or an intrusion? *(Oh, hi Lord. Pull up a chair. I'll be right with you. I just need to catch the last fifteen minutes of "American Idol.")*

Because of the love between this family and Jesus, it was completely understandable that when Lazarus became seriously ill, they immediately sent word to the Lord. They knew Jesus would care and be concerned. And the fact is, He cared very much and was deeply concerned. But He didn't respond like they thought He would to the news of His friend's serious illness. Not at all.

> Now a certain man was sick, Lazarus of Bethany, the town of Mary and her sister Martha. It was that Mary who anointed the Lord with fragrant oil and wiped His feet with her hair, whose brother Lazarus was sick. Therefore the sisters sent to Him, saying, "Lord, behold, he whom You love is sick." (vv. 1–3)

This wasn't an invitation. It wasn't a request. They didn't say, "Lord, please come!" They simply made some assumptions. Knowing how Jesus loved their family, they assumed that as soon as He learned of the situation, He would drop whatever He was doing and hurry to His friend's bedside.

Mary and Martha provide us with an excellent example of what to do when we or others are sick or are in need. We call on the Lord…but we don't necessarily tell Him what He should do. There's nothing wrong in asking for the removal of your problem, or the healing of your loved one. But it should always be in the context of "Not our will, but Yours be done," as Jesus taught us.

Even so, we should always bring our troubles to Jesus. When the Israelites criticized and turned against Moses, "He cried out to the Lord" (Exodus 15:25).

When King Hezekiah received a troubling, threatening letter, he "went up to the house of the Lord, and spread it before the Lord" (Isaiah 37:14).

When John the Baptist was beheaded in prison, his disciples "went and told Jesus" (Matthew 14:12).

And that's just what we need to do at the first sign of trouble. Go and tell Jesus. Scripture tells us that "He is a very present help in trouble" (Psalm 46:1).

"Lord, behold, he whom You love is sick."

Note the basis for their appeal. Was it because they had hosted Him in their home and invited Him over for so many meals? Were they counting on the fact that "He owed them," and would return a favor for favors given?

No, the basis of the appeal was simply love. He loved them. They loved Him. And people who love one another care for one another.

But a couple of verses later, something perplexing—and very significant—happened when Jesus received their appeal.

> Now Jesus loved Martha and her sister and Lazarus, therefore when He heard that he was sick He stayed two more days in the place where He was. (v. 5)

In other words, He was seemingly late, and had a reason for it.

And that reason was love.

"WHERE WERE YOU, LORD?"

Scripture says clearly that Jesus delayed His arrival to Bethany because He loved Lazarus and his sisters.

What? Isn't that a contradiction? *If Jesus really loved Lazarus why didn't He immediately go and heal him?* And when hardship and tragedy enter our lives, we might ask the same. *"If Jesus really loved me, why did He let this happen?"*

It's hard to see through eyes filled with tears. The point is, even though we can't see how the situation will end or why it has come upon us, we can know it flows from the love of God and falls under His control.

We must interpret His delays, then—or those things that seem to be delays from our perspective—in the light of His love. And not the other way around.

> Now Martha, as soon as she heard that Jesus was coming, went and met Him, but Mary was sitting in the house. Now Martha said to Jesus, "Lord, if You had been here, my brother would not have died. But even now I know that whatever You ask of God, God will give You."

> Jesus said to her, "Your brother will rise again."

> Martha said to Him, "I know that he will rise again in the resurrection at the last day."

> Jesus said to her, "I am the resurrection and the life. He who believes in Me, though he may die, he shall live. And whoever lives

and believes in Me shall never die. Do you believe this?" She said to Him, "Yes, Lord, I believe that You are the Christ, the Son of God, who is to come into the world."

And when she had said these things, she went her way and secretly called Mary her sister, saying, "The Teacher has come and is calling for you." (vv. 20–28)

Martha couldn't hide her feelings of hurt and devastation. *"Lord, if You had been here [if You had been on time], my brother would not have died."* Pretty brash words. Have you ever felt that way?

Where were You, Lord?

Where were You when my loved one died?

Where were You when I was being abused?

Where were You when my marriage dissolved?

Where were You when my parents divorced?

Where were You when my child went astray?

Notice that Jesus did not reprove Martha for what she said. It's not sinful to tell God how you feel. Just look at the psalms, where time and again David cries out his hurts, his doubts, his frustrations, and his sorrow. It's not wrong to verbalize your doubts. Just make sure you take time to listen to His response!

Instead of correcting Martha for making this statement, Jesus sought to bring her back to an eternal perspective. In fact, Jesus wanted to do above and beyond what Mary and Martha could imagine.

They wanted a healing; He wanted a resurrection.

They only thought of friendship; He of the ultimate sacrificial love.

They had their hearts fixed on temporal comfort; He was thinking of eternal comfort.

Why do we human beings tend to think this way? Because in our minds, the "worse case scenario" is to die. How could this possibly be the will of God?

That's only a difficult question because of where we place most of our focus...on this side of eternity. We don't see the Big Picture. We focus on that micro-thin slice of time—our few years here on earth—rather than the endless morning of eternity. We are interested in that which benefits us temporally, while God is interested in what benefits us forever and ever.

There are some things we will simply never

understand when God allows a tragedy or difficulty or even the death of a loved one. Paul wrote, "For our present troubles are quite small and won't last very long. Yet they produce for us an immeasurably great glory that will last forever!" (2 Corinthians 4:17, NLT).

What is that glory? What does it look like, feel like, taste like? We can't know on this side of life. But we have the word of God Himself that it will be "immeasurably great" and "will last forever."

I don't know about you…but that's good enough for me.

Jesus wanted to do *more* than Mary and Martha asked Him to. We must remember to not limit the Lord in our times of prayer. We think we know exactly what He should do…or sometimes we give Him options in our prayers, telling Him that either A, B, or maybe even C would be acceptable outcomes. But God may be thinking on a completely different level altogether, far beyond our comprehension or imagination. The Bible tells us that "by his mighty power at work within us, he is able to accomplish infinitely more than we would ever dare to ask or hope" (Ephesians 3:20, NLT).

That's why it is never dangerous to fully yield

to His will. It may not be until the very end of our lives that we will be able to see the Lord's wisdom and plan unfolding in our lives. Then again, it may not be until we are in eternity looking into the very face of Jesus.

Until then we must trust Him.

Until then, we must leave the timing of His answers to our prayers in His hands. From our perspective, He may seem unresponsive at times. He may seem to have forgotten our pain, forgotten our dilemma, forgotten our struggle.

But it isn't so. God is never late. He is always on time. The One who created time and set it in motion will never be frustrated, limited, or defeated by that which He created.

David, who endured so many highs and lows in his life, had to come to the place where he simply released all the details—all his hopes and dreams and desires—into the Lord's hands. He wrote in Psalm 31:14–15: "But as for me, I trust in You, O Lord; I say, 'You are my God.' My times are in Your hand."

WHEN TIMES GET HOT

Do you think those three Hebrew teenagers,

Shadrach, Meshach and Abed-nego would have
been able to quote that psalm, and say "My times
are in Your hand"? Do you think they might have
been tempted to think God forgot about them?

You remember the story from the book of
Daniel. The king of Babylon gave a decree that
all should bow before his golden image or die in a
blazing furnace of fire. Nebuchadnezzar wasn't into
religious tolerance. He had no interest in diversity.
For him, politically correct meant "what I say." So
when the specified "theme music" was played all
across the land, the people obediently fell prostrate
before the image of the egotistical ruler.

Everyone, that is, except the three Hebrew holy
boys, Shadrach, Meshach and Abed-nego. And
when everyone in the whole kingdom has fallen
on their face and you're still vertical, you tend to
stand out a little. The king was so enraged by their
non-compliance that he commanded the fire to
be heated seven times hotter! It was so severe it
overcame the very guards given the unpleasant task
of throwing them in!

The young men were given one more chance
to change their minds. But they would not. *Where
was God?* Why didn't He come and scorch this

idolatrous king and his followers?

Where was God?

He was waiting for them in the furnace.

For when they were finally thrown in, much to Nebuchadnezzar's surprise, he "saw four of them in there walking around, and the fourth was like the Son of God" (Daniel 3:25).

Sometimes God delivers us *from* the trial.

Sometimes He delivers us *in* it.

God received more glory by letting them go through the experience than He would have received if they had never gone through the flames at all. And they would have never seen with their own eyes how the Lord would walk with them right in the midst of an inferno! This wasn't the kind of lesson they were likely to forget about. And no matter what happened to these men for the rest of their lives, no matter what trials or traumas crossed their path, they had already seen God deliver them from the flames. What circumstance could compare with that?

"THE LAST MINUTE"

Then there's the story of the Israelite nation crossing the Red Sea. Moses had demanded the release of the captive Israelites from Egypt time and time again, but the Pharaoh resisted, making their slave existence even harder than ever.

Finally, after God's judgment fell (and fell and fell and fell), Pharaoh relented and let the people go. Joy filled their hearts as they began their massive exodus out of Egypt, on their way to a wonderful promised land. But soon they realized a major obstacle was before them...the Red Sea. Now what? Were they trapped?

Where was God? Was He going to show up on time?

The Bible says, "Then Moses raised his hand over the sea, and the LORD opened up a path through the water with a strong east wind. The wind blew all that night, turning the seabed into dry land. So the people of Israel walked through the sea on dry ground, with walls of water on each side!" (Exodus 14:21, NLT).

No one had ever seen anything like it! An ocean, parting down the middle? A dry pathway through the very midst of the sea, with huge walls of hovering water on each side? Who could pull that off but Almighty God?

Just *before* the sea had parted, however, the

people were in a panic. The sea was before them, and behind them the Egyptian army, spears and swords glinting in the sunlight, was thundering toward them in their chariots.

As the enemy drew closer and closer, the people of God thought all was lost.

But then God came through.

And guess when?

"During the last watch of the night [or the 'fourth watch'] the LORD looked down from the pillar of fire and cloud at the Egyptian army and threw it into confusion. Their chariot wheels began to come off, making their chariots impossible to drive. 'Let's get out of here!' the Egyptians shouted. 'The Lord is fighting for Israel against us!'" (cf. Exodus 14:24–25).

Then the waters closed back in, drowning the entire Egyptian army.

The Fourth Watch. The last minute. We may find ourselves walking very, very close to the edge in this life of faith, but the edge isn't such a bad place to be. You can see a lot from the edge. And one of the things you will see is that God is never late. He is always on time.

As we look at our world around us right now we

wonder, "How long, O Lord, 'till You return to this earth?" We see horrible violence and perversion. People not only breaking God's laws, but flaunting their wicked lifestyles. When will He come again?

Peter tells us a bit about God's perfect timing when he writes:

> First, I want to remind you that in the last days there will be scoffers who will laugh at the truth and do every evil thing they desire. This will be their argument: "Jesus promised to come back, did he? Then where is he? Why, as far back as anyone can remember, everything has remained exactly the same since the world was first created." …The Lord isn't really being slow about his promise to return, as some people think. No, he is being patient for your sake. He does not want anyone to perish, so he is giving more time for everyone to repent.
> (2 Peter 3:3–4, 9, NLT)

Does it seem late to you right now? It does to me. Listen to what the Bible says about that:

"The night is far spent, the day is at hand. Therefore let us cast off the works of darkness, and let us put on the armor of light. Let us walk properly, as in the day, not in revelry and drunkenness, not in lewdness and lust, not in strife and envy. But put on the Lord Jesus Christ, and make no provision for the flesh, to fulfill its lusts" (Romans 13:12).

J. B. Phillips translates this verse with these dramatic words: "The night is nearly over, the day has almost dawned, let us therefore fling away the things that men do in the dark! Let us arm ourselves for the fight of the day. Let us live cleanly, as in the daylight, not in the 'delights' of getting drunk or playing with sex nor in quarreling or jealousies. Let us be Christ's men from head to foot and give no chances to the flesh to have its fling!"

Remember, the Fourth Watch is that time right before the rising of the sun.

He is coming again, and He is right on time.

I heard the story of a little boy who was visiting his grandparents' house and was lying on the living room floor playing with his toys. There in the front room was a large, old-fashioned grandfather clock.

Noontime was getting close and, as he always did, the little boy counted the chimes until it hit 12. On this particular day, however, something malfunctioned inside the clock's inner mechanism.

Instead of stopping at 12, it kept right on chiming, *13-14-15-16 times.* The boy couldn't believe his ears! He jumped to his feet and ran into the kitchen, shouting, *"Grandma! Grandma! It's later than it's ever been before!"*

And so it is. It's never been this "late" in the history of our troubled planet. We've never been closer to the darkest of nights...or the brightest of dawns.

How to Overcome
Temptation

> God blesses the people who patiently endure testing. Afterward they will receive the crown of life that God has promised to those who love him. And remember, no one who wants to do wrong should ever say, "God is tempting me." God is never tempted to do wrong, and he never tempts anyone else either. Temptation comes from the lure of our own evil desires. These evil desires lead to evil actions, and evil actions lead to death. So don't be misled, my dear brothers and sisters. (James 1:12–16, NLT)

Temptation is a little like an eccentric relative who lives next door.

Like him or not, he's a familiar visitor in your life. You might want him to go away for a long time, you might long for him to just leave you alone, or—in your worst moments—you might even wish he didn't even exist. But wanting, longing, and wishing won't change the reality of your situation. You're going to have to learn how to deal with him.

All of us know about temptation, and none of us like it. Yet it is a reality of life on this fallen planet, for believer and nonbeliever alike.

But it may surprise you to know that testing and even temptation can have a positive effect in your life. It has been said that "Christians are a lot like teabags. You don't know what they're made of until you put them in hot water."

Everyone faces temptation in one way, shape, or form on a daily basis. And may I shock you for a moment? That includes ministers! I heard the story of a minister who parked his car in a no parking zone in a large city. He was short on time, had an important appointment, and simply could not find a space.

In desperation, he put a note under the windshield wiper which read: *"I have circled the block ten times! I have an appointment to keep. 'Forgive us our trespasses.'"*

When the pastor returned, he found a citation from a police officer, along with this note: *"I've circled this block for ten years! If I don't give you a ticket, I lose my job! 'Lead us not into temptation.'*"

In this chapter, we will look at the following aspects of temptation:

- · Where does it come from?
- · When does it come?
- · To whom does it come?
- · How does it come?
- · How do I resist it when it comes?

WHERE DOES TEMPTATION COME FROM?

But each one is tempted when he is drawn away by his own desires… (James 1:14).

We would like to think that temptation is some irresistible force that suddenly descends upon us and knocks us off our feet. But it isn't so. In one sense, temptation is an inside job. For the enemy to succeed he needs some cooperation.

Without question we clearly play a part in our own temptation. Where there is no desire on our part, then there is no temptation. The flesh with its evil desires is the internal foe. Satan with his enticements is the external foe.

Verse 14 tells us that each one is drawn away *by his own desires*. The trouble lies in the "combustible material each man carries within himself."

Jesus also told us, "Not what goes into the mouth defiles a man; but what comes out of the mouth, this defiles a man" (Matthew 15:11). In other words—those things that come forth from within him, from his heart. Paul added, "Don't you know that when you offer yourselves to someone to obey him as slaves, you are slaves to the one whom you obey—whether you are slaves to sin, which leads to death, or to obedience, which leads to righteousness?" (Romans 6:16, NIV).

We play a key role in our own temptation.

When my son Jonathan was still very young, I sent him to bed one night with some clear instructions. "Now turn off the light, Jonathan. And no more video games, okay?"

"Okay, Dad."

Just a little while later, however, I noticed a familiar blue glow coming from beneath his bedroom door. Throwing it open, I caught little Jonathan red-handed, blasting away at enemy space ships. When I demanded an explanation, he blurted out, "Dad, I didn't *mean* to. But I couldn't resist myself!"

It was so cute that I just let it go that time (after unplugging the video game). But I think my little boy was onto something. We love to blame the devil and others for our spiritual stumbles and falls. But the truth is, we just can't resist ourselves.

Sometimes we even want to blame God for our missteps. We will lamely say something along the lines of, "God just gave me more than I could handle!" Talk about passing the buck! This is exactly what our ancestor Adam did in the Garden, when he blamed his wife (who happened to be the only other person on the planet) for luring him into sin. It's what we do when we can't own up to our own complicity in our sinful choices.

The Bible clearly refutes this kind of thinking, reminding us, "Let no one say when he is tempted, 'I am tempted by God'; for God cannot be tempted by evil, nor does He Himself tempt anyone" (James 1:13).

This reminds me of the fable of the scorpion and the turtle. As you may or may not know, scorpions can't swim. So one day a scorpion who wanted to cross a pond found a turtle basking in the summer sun, and asked if he would give him a lift across the pond.

"Are you joking?" the turtle exclaimed. "You'll *sting* me while I'm swimming, and I'll drown."

"My dear turtle," laughed the scorpion, "If I were to sting you, you *would* drown—but I'd go down with you. Now where is the logic in that?"

"You've got a point there," reasoned the turtle. "Hop on."

The scorpion climbed aboard, and halfway across the pond he carefully aimed his powerful stinger at the turtle's vulnerable neck and gave him everything he had.

At that, they both began to sink. Resigned to his fate, the turtle turned to the scorpion and said, "Do you mind if I ask you something? You said there was no logic in your stinging me. Why did you do it?"

"It has nothing to do with logic," the drowning scorpion replied. "It's just my nature!"

That's a fairly accurate way of defining temptation. When we get tempted and yield to it, we like to lay the blame at the feet of someone or something else. *"The devil made me do it,"* we say. Or maybe, *"That person trapped me. I'm not responsible."*

But the fact of the matter is, "it's just our nature."

Or, as that great eleven-year-old theologian Jonathan Laurie said, "I couldn't resist myself."

Remember, it's the world, the flesh, and the devil working in concert together. Our "contribution" to the process is our own sinful flesh. We play a key role in our own temptation.

WHEN DOES THE TEMPTATION COME?

Surprisingly enough, temptation often comes after times of great blessing.

Sometimes we talk about a "mountaintop experience" after being at a camp or a conference or an exciting worship service. Think of what a great moment it must have been for the young Carpenter of Nazareth when His cousin John baptized Him in the muddy waters of the Jordan River. After coming up out of the water, one translation says He saw the heavens "torn open."

Wow! The fabric of sky somehow parted and He saw "the Spirit descending upon Him like a dove. Then a voice came from heaven, 'You are My beloved Son, in whom I am well pleased'" (Mark 1:10–11).

Now *that* is a spiritual high. I've had some pretty amazing worship and prayer experiences in my life, but how can you top this one? The sky parting, the heavens torn open, the Holy Spirit descending in visible form, a voice from the Throne of Glory, saying, *"You're My own Son. I love You with all My heart, and I'm so pleased with You."*

That's not a little hilltop kind of spiritual experience, that's Mount Everest! But even Jesus wasn't allowed to stay there very long. The Bible tells us that "Immediately the Spirit drove Him into the wilderness. And He was there in the wilderness forty days, tempted by Satan, and was with the wild beasts" (Mark 1:12–13). He began a forty-day fast out there in the incredibly desolate and hostile land. And at the end of it, He was weak and hungry. *That* was the moment Satan chose to launch a direct, frontal assault.

It must have seemed a long way from that golden moment of His baptism and the affirming voice of His Father, echoing off the hills like the thunder. It would be like stepping off a cliff with a hang glider, soaring straight up about a thousand feet, then dropping like a stone.

But that's the way it is sometimes—for all of us. As believers, we're privileged to enjoy some extraordinary times of rich teaching, wonderful fellowship, and soul-stretching music. God pours His grace and favor into our lives at such times, and we feel a surge of spiritual strength and joy.

Great! Soak it up. Savor every moment of it. But know this. The devil and his demon army choose the time and place of attack—and oftentimes it is after a season of great blessing.

History tells us that when Hitler invaded the European nations during the early years of World War Two, in almost every situation he attacked on a weekend. The dictator knew that across Europe, various Parliaments would not be in session, making it more difficult to react swiftly to a lightning invasion.

In the same way, our enemy the devil waits for the most opportune time to hit us with temptation. He waits for that moment when we are the most vulnerable. And when is that? It may very well be when we think we are the strongest! Scripture says, "So, if you think you are standing firm, be careful that you don't fall!" (1 Corinthians 10:12, NIV).

TO WHOM DOES TEMPTATION COME?

In a broad sense, everyone is tempted. At the same time, without question, the Enemy focuses his attacks on those who are young in the faith, and those who are making a difference in the Kingdom.

Most of us can remember those days shortly after we came to Christ, when temptation hit us with a fresh intensity. Or maybe the Enemy was trying to play with our minds, tempting us to doubt that God had truly forgiven us. It was like Satan's first temptation of Eve, in the Garden, when he whispered, *"Has God indeed said…?"* And after planting the doubts about God in our minds, Satan tries to pull us back into the old life again.

Whenever we have the opportunity to lead someone to Jesus Christ, we need to warn that new convert that he or she has just become a prime target of the evil one. In Mark 4:15, Jesus spoke of "the ones by the wayside where the word is sown. When they hear, Satan comes immediately and takes away the word that was sown in their hearts."

Just a few days after I received Christ as a young high school student, I ran right into a major temptation in my life. I was so excited—really just bubbling over—about what God had done for me. I even wore a little button on my shirt with a drawing of Jesus on it.

In one of my classes one day, I noticed a very

attractive girl looking at me and smiling. Now, I had noticed this girl before (I wasn't blind), but frankly, she had never noticed me. And now, seemingly out of nowhere, she was making eyes at me!

But the Christians I had just met had already warned me. They told me not to be surprised if I ran into some strong temptations soon after inviting Jesus to be my Lord. And I remember wondering in that moment, *Could this be it?* I didn't have to wait long to find out, because just as class let out, that cute little dish sashayed up to me and said, "Hi. What's your name?"

I forgot my name momentarily, I was so stunned by her sudden interest in me.

"I'm Greg," I finally managed to say.

"You're cute, Greg," she cooed. "I've never noticed you before."

Truthfully, I was dumbfounded. You have to project yourself back into adolescence to get a handle on what an effect an encounter like this could have on a teenage boy.

Then she looked into my eyes with those cornflower blue eyes of hers and said, "I'd really like to get to know you better. Hey…my parents have this house up in the mountains, and they'll be gone this weekend. Want to go up with me?"

I knew this had to be a temptation, just like my friends warned me, because things like this just don't happen to me! I thought to myself, *Why is this happening to me now when I can't act on it? Talk about bad timing!*

Then it dawned on me.

It wasn't bad timing. It was precise timing. From hell. Satan was hitting me where I was weak and when I was young in the faith. And in that moment, I remember getting excited. Not about the temptation, but about the opportunity to resist! I remember thinking to myself, *If Satan wants to trip me up this much, God must have something really special in store for me.* So, by the grace of God, I said no to her, and she walked off in a huff. (I'm sure she quickly found another taker for her little mountain getaway.)

I felt a great sense of relief and joy. As a new follower of Jesus Christ, I had made my first conscious decision to turn away from what I very much wanted to do. And I was blessed, or happy, as James 1:12 tells us we will be when we resist temptation.

Then, besides the young in the faith, Satan and his legions also want to cut the legs out from under those who are making a difference in the kingdom. Charles Spurgeon once observed, "You don't kick a dead horse!"

Why did Satan tempt Samson, David, Solomon, Joseph, and Peter? Because of the *damage* they were all doing to his kingdom of darkness. They had his attention! (And notice that in three out of the four cases, he used sex as bait in his trap. That should tell us something!)

So when you say (as you certainly should say), "Use me Lord, let my life make a difference!" *brace yourself.* The Enemy won't take this sitting down. Don't expect a standing ovation in hell.

HOW DOES TEMPTATION COME?

In many if not most cases, temptation enters through the doorway of the mind. When Satan wanted to lead the first man and woman into sin, he began by attacking the woman's mind.

In the New Testament, Paul elaborates with these words: "I am afraid, lest as the serpent deceived Eve by his craftiness, your minds should be led astray from the simplicity and purity of devotion to Christ" (2 Corinthians 11:3).

Why does Satan attack the believer's mind?

Because it is here we reason, contemplate, speculate, and fantasize. Paul wrote about the battle that often rages within our minds—assuring us of the great victory we can enjoy in Jesus.

> The weapons we fight with are not the weapons of the world. On the contrary, they have divine power to demolish strongholds. We demolish arguments and every pretension that sets itself up against the knowledge of God, and we take captive every thought to make it obedient to Christ. (2 Corinthians 10:4–5, NIV)

Your mind can reach into the past through memories, and into the future through imagination, drawing you to speculate, *What if…? What would it be like if…?*

For Israel, the big problem was looking in the rearview mirror. As God led the nation through the wilderness en route to the Promised Land, the people started thinking about "the good old days," back in Egypt. They remembered the "garlics, leeks, and onions" they used to throw in the crock pot, and no longer valued God's miraculous provision of manna, the bread from heaven.

"Good old Egypt?" Are you kidding, Israel?

You were slaves! You were pushed by ruthless slave-drivers cracking the whip across your backs. Your baby sons were sent to their deaths by command of the Pharaoh. You had no opportunity, no hope, no future. Yet even as they enjoyed God's miraculous provision, they let their minds run wild. In their fevered imaginations, they somehow turned a slave diet into an Egyptian banquet, full of tasty delights.

They apparently had forgotten about the cruelty of their forced labor, and their constant cries for a deliverer.

The first step to *going* back—back to the old life, back to the old ways—is *looking back*. And we do that through our thoughts. Have you been doing that lately?

There's no denying the magnetic lure of temptation. It can be very strong. At times, it can seem irresistible. And Satan is no fool. He's not going to tell you what his ultimate goal is by throwing those temptations into your path. His poison is generally dipped in fine chocolate—initially tasty, then deadly.

When Eve was tempted by the Tree, she looked at that fruit and said to herself, *It's pleasing to my eyes…. It's good for food.* In other words, never mind about the consequences or long-range effects. (I'll think about that tomorrow.) It's going to satisfy a desire I have right here and now.

This is the tricky thing about temptation. It's intoxicating. It titillated her senses and was a pleasurable experience. When sin has you in its grip, you begin to rationalize your behavior.

"I'll know when to stop."

"It has a thirty-day money back guarantee!"

"Everyone's doing it."

You can speculate all you want about "what you would do" in a tempting situation, but it's very different when you actually find yourself in the heat of the moment.

· …*When Achan saw the bar of gold, the bag of silver, and a beautiful Babylonian garment in the ruins of Jericho (Joshua 7:21).*

· …*When Potiphar's lustful wife grabbed young Joseph by the coat and said, "Come to bed with me!" (Genesis 40:7).*

· …*When David took the evening walk on his palace roof and saw what he hadn't intended to see, and stayed longer than he'd intended to stay (2 Samuel 11:2–3).*

· *...When Demas turned his back on a crucial ministry to Paul in the apostle's greatest hour of need (2 Timothy 4:10).*

Until you find yourself in the actual situation, you have no idea how tempting "tempting" will be. That's why all of us need to be alert and prepared all of the time.

WHERE IS THE BEST PLACE TO BE WHEN TEMPTATION COMES?

The best and safest place to be is in the will of God.

Scripture tells us that Jesus was "led *by the Spirit* into the wilderness" where He was tempted by the devil. Yes, He was being tempted. But He was also squarely in the bull's eye of God's will.

Far too often we allow ourselves to drift away from the will of God, essentially bringing temptation upon ourselves. What makes resisting temptation difficult for many people is that they don't want to completely discourage it. Most people say they want to be delivered from temptation...but would like to "keep in touch." To send temptation away, but first get its cell number. To pray against evil influences, and yet rush into places of danger. To thrust their fingers into the fire, and then pray that they might not be burned.

Peter, warming himself by the enemy's fire, certainly was out of the will of God. As with Eve at the tree of the knowledge of good and evil, the big fisherman was at the wrong place, listening to the wrong voice, that led him to do the wrong thing... that absolutely devastated his heart.

WHAT IS THE BEST TOOL FOR RESISTING TEMPTATION?

The Word of God!

During the time of the Lord's temptation, Satan transported Him to the pinnacle of the temple, and told Him, "Jump off! If You are God's Son, His angels will protect You!"

But Jesus knew the book: "*It is written*, you shall not put the Lord your God to the test" (Matthew 4:7, NIV).

Christ was "rightly dividing the word of truth." He did not use "executive privilege" as God's Son, but instead gave us the model of winning skirmishes and out-and-out battles in spiritual warfare by depending on the Word of God and the Spirit of God alone.

We can't expect to turn back a powerful enemy with no weapon in our hand. You wouldn't see a U.S. Marine in Iraq patrolling the streets of Baghdad with only a newspaper in his hands. You wouldn't expect an ATF agent to kick down the door of a drug house armed with only his Daytimer.

And neither does God expect us to walk empty-handed into spiritual warfare with a fierce and crafty enemy. Ephesians 6:17 tells us, "Take the helmet of salvation, and the sword of the Spirit, which is the word of God." All of the pieces of armor described in the sixth chapter of Ephesians are *defensive*.

All except this one—which is both.

If as a believer you do not have a good "working knowledge" of Scripture, you will surely become a casualty in the spiritual battle that rages around us every day. Really, it's only a matter of time. Once the enemy realizes you are weaponless, he will launch every flaming arrow in his arsenal—straight at your heart and mind.

A warrior takes care of his weapon, knowing his life and the lives of others may depend upon it. What shape is your sword in? Is it polished from daily use as you study the Scripture? Is it sharpened on the anvil of experience as you have applied and obeyed its truth in your life? Or is it rusty from lack of preparation or dulled by disobedience?

Satan will do everything he can to keep you from the Book. (As he did with Eve, first questioning it, then distorting it, and finally adding to it.) When people on occasion ask me to sign their Bibles, I usually write what D. L. Moody once wrote: "This book will keep you from sin, or sin will keep you from this book."

It doesn't matter if you are a brand new child of God or a seasoned believer who has walked with Him for decades, *success or failure in the Christian life depends on how much of the Bible you get into your heart and mind on a regular basis, and how faithful you are to obey it.* If we neglect the study of the Scripture, our spiritual life will ultimately unravel, because everything we need to know about God and life is taught in the Bible. And if it can't be found in the pages of Scripture you don't need it! If it's "new," then it's not true. If it's true, then it's not new.

Every believer must make it a top priority to memorize the Word of God. We often forget what we ought to remember, and remember what we ought to forget. To this day, I have memory banks that are still filled with obscure Beatles' lyrics and old TV commercials.

SWORD AT THE READY

We need to make a conscious effort to keep the Word of God at the forefront of our hearts and minds. It's good to carry a Bible in your briefcase, pocket, or purse, but the best place to carry it is in your heart. If you have it in your heart, no one can ever take it away from you. In the book of Deuteronomy, the Lord tells His people to "commit yourselves completely to these words of mine. Tie them to your hands as a reminder, and wear them on your forehead. Teach them to your children. Talk about them when you are at home and when you are away on a journey, when you are lying down and when you are getting up again. Write them on the doorposts of your house and on your gates" (Deuteronomy 11:18–20, NLT).

Once Scripture becomes ingrained in your memory, it will always be there for you. There will be times when that word you memorized will pay great dividends. It will bring comfort to your heart, and needed strength in a time of intense temptation or spiritual attack.

In the same way, having God's Word near to

hand can help us stand against temptation. The psalmist wrote, "Your word I have hidden in my heart, that I might not sin against You" (Psalm 119:11). And in Psalm 37, David writes: "The law of God is in his heart; his steps do not slip."

Our minds should be so saturated with His Word that they will be like "spiritual computers." When we find ourselves facing crucial decisions, spiritual warfare, or red-hot temptations, we automatically remember the Scriptures that relate to that particular situation.

It is the ministry of the Holy Spirit to bring God's Word to our minds when we need it. In John 14:26, Jesus said, "But the Counselor, the Holy Spirit, whom the Father will send in My name, will teach you all things and will remind you of everything I have said to you." But we shouldn't expect the Spirit to remind us of something we have never learned!

FIGHTING *FROM* VICTORY

Here is an important foundational truth to remember when it comes to temptation. We do not fight for victory but *from* it. The battle has already been won by Jesus Christ at the cross. Prior to His crucifixion, Jesus said, "Now is the judgment of this world: now shall the prince of this world be cast out" (John 12:31).

Through that death on the cross, Jesus destroyed "him that had the power of death, that is, the devil" (Hebrews 2:14). Paul explains even further in his letter to Colosse: "Having canceled the written code, with its regulations, that was against us and that stood opposed to us; he took it away, nailing it to the cross. And having disarmed the powers and authorities, he made a public spectacle of them, triumphing over them by the cross" (Colossians 2:14–15, NIV).

You might ask, "If Jesus' death at Calvary was powerful and complete, why do we still see Satan on the scene doing his dirty work?"

Why? *Because God has allowed it.* That's not a cop-out. It's simply a recognition of a temporary situation. Even so, remember that the Enemy does nothing in the life of the Christian without the permission of God.

As I said, temptation is allowed and even used by God.

We all know what can happen when an individual gives in to temptation. We see its devastating effect on many in Scripture as well as people we know (not to mention ourselves). James 1:15 says that "when desire has conceived, it gives birth to sin." It is an absolute law of God that we will reap what we sow. Verse 16 literally tells us, "Stop being deceived about this!" Don't allow yourself to be led astray and wander from the truth.

Trials, testings, and temptations will come whether we want them to or not. And it is the Word of God "hidden in your heart" that will restrain you from sinning against the very One who loves you most.

The key is what we do with these testings (from God) and temptations (from the enemy, but allowed by God). A. B. Simpson wrote: "Temptation exercises our faith and teaches us to pray. It is like military drill and a taste of battle to the young soldier. It puts us under fire and compels us to exercise our weapons and prove their potency. It shows us the recourse of Christ and the preciousness of the promises of God. Every victory gives us new confidence in our victorious Leader and new courage for the next onslaught of the foe." With Paul, we step up to the line of battle "with weapons of righteousness in the right hand and in the left" (2 Corinthians 6:7, NIV).

In the Amplified Bible, James 1:12 reads: "Blessed (happy, to be envied) is the man who is patient under trial and stands up under temptation, for when he has stood the test and been approved, he will receive [the victor's] crown of life which God has promised to those who love Him."

No, it's not easy at the time. No one said the Christian life would be easy. But what a great blessing there is in knowing you passed the test. If we really want to follow God we will cling to Him all the tighter, and like Joseph running from Potiphar's wife, we will "flee from temptation"— even if we have to leave our coat behind. It's better than our hide!

If we don't take those steps, we may very well let go and fall.

And once you fall, who can say how far you will fall or what damage will be done to God's great plans for your life? Who can calculate the opportunities and blessings you will miss when you have refused to follow the path of life?

Where then, does temptation come from? "From our own passions...." Or as the scorpion in the fable said, "It's just my nature."

When does it come?

Often after times of great blessing in our lives, or

when we may feel we are invulnerable. Many times when we least expect it. So keep your guard up!

To whom does it come?

In a general sense, to everyone. Yet Satan clearly sets his sights on those he considers young and vulnerable in the faith or those who become a particular threat to his turf and domain.

How does it come?

Most often in realm of our thoughts.

Where is the best place to be when it comes? Smack dab in the middle of the will of God, as close to Him as possible.

Finally, what is the best tool we have to resist temptation?

The sword of the Spirit, which is the Word of God.

Temptation will be our lot in life as long as we walk about on the surface of this planet. But there will come a day, as we step from this life into the next, that temptation will fade away like a bad dream in the light of a new morning.

How to Know the
Will of God

DOES GOD STILL SPEAK TO MAN TODAY?

I s He interested in what happens to us as individuals? Does He really have a master plan for our lives? If so, how do I discover it? How do I hear His voice? How do I know the will of God?

These are important questions…and not easily answered. We all need guidance concerning the great questions of life. *Who should I marry? Should I make a certain move? How does God want me to serve Him with my life?*

The answer to the first question, "Does God still speak to man today?" is an unqualified *yes*! We as Christians are not "victims of chance," blindly feeling our way along life's maze, hoping our luck won't run out or we won't run into a dead end. Just as God led men and women throughout the pages of Scripture, so He wants to lead us.

But *how?* you ask. How does it happen? How will I know?

I wish I could give you an easy "1-2-3" method on how to discover the will of God in every life situation. But in my walk with Jesus Christ of thirty-plus years, I have found that the will of God unfolded in my life—one decision at a time—as I took steps of faith, trying to the best of my ability to live by the principles of Scripture.

Yes, there have been those times when He has spoken to me in a rather tangible way, but most of the time it has been a journey of faith.

And that is what the Scripture tells us again and again: *"The just shall live by faith."* As we will see, God's will is not an itinerary, but an attitude.

JUST START WALKING

Clearly, God is vitally interested in the lives of His sons and daughters. He does speak. He delights to guide and counsel. And in this chapter we will briefly examine some of these principles of guidance. God does not play hide-and-seek. He wants to lead you even more than you want to be led. God is more concerned about keeping us in

His will than we are to be kept in it!

Far too often, we can make knowing God's will seem mystical, "other-worldly"—almost spooky. When I hear some preachers talking about their extended, audible conversations with the Lord, I tend to think a lot of it is coming from their fertile imagination...or worse! Speaking of those who falsely represent Him, the Lord said through Ezekiel: "And your prophets announce false visions and speak false messages. They say, 'My message is from the Sovereign LORD,' when the LORD hasn't spoken a single word to them" (Ezekiel 22:28).

Though God may not necessarily speak to us like you would speak to your neighbor over the back fence, He is very interested in showing us His desire and purpose for our lives day by day. And I have found that there are concrete, practical steps that I can take to more easily discern and follow God's will.

God's way becomes plain when we start walking in it! God said of Abraham, "Shall I hide from Abraham the thing I am about to do?" He wanted to reveal His purposes to Abraham and Sarah. In fact, Abraham was called the "friend of God." We have that privilege, too. In John 15:15, the Lord Jesus said, "I no longer call you servants, because a servant does not know his master's business. Instead, I have called you friends, for everything that I learned from my Father I have made known to you."

Friends share secrets with friends. They confide in them. They open their hearts to them. Scripture says, "The secret of the LORD is with those who fear Him" (Psalm 25:14). That's important, because there are many voices calling you to go this way or that way.

Jesus said, "My sheep hear My voice." But many of these other voices will lead you astray. You need to know God's will and way for your life. He is the One who says, "This is the way, walk ye in it" (Isaiah 30:21, KJV).

As I mentioned, Jesus describes Himself as the Good Shepherd and us as His sheep. And He says, "My sheep hear My voice and *follow*." Is that the case with you today? Are you hearing His voice? Just as importantly, are you following it?

Did you know that there are passages in Scripture that declare God's will for you at this very moment? Perhaps one thing He is waiting for before He reveals the specific plans He has for you is for you to act on what He has already clearly revealed as plain as day in the pages of the Bible. We may find ourselves crying out to God, "Show me Your will, show me Your will!" while holding the answer right in our hands.

Let's say you were having a problem programming your new DVD player. So you tell yourself, "I need the people at Sony Electronics to transmit a special message to my mind right now!" No, you need to open up the pesky little thing called a "User's Manual" and read it. And then you need to actually do what it tells you to do. (If you're like me, you try to find people to read them for you and then explain it.)

We need to look at what God has already declared in His *"User's Manual."* We won't look at these passages in depth, but rather to get a sense of some specific things the Scriptures reveal as the will of God for our lives…right now.

Obedience to revealed truth guarantees guidance in matters unrevealed.

The first one will seem obvious…but we can't miss it. Otherwise, all the others are of no real value. *Are you ready to know God's will? Here it comes!*

#1: You must be a believer.

The Scripture says that God will have "all men to be saved…" (1 Timothy 2:4). "God is not willing that any should perish but that all should come to repentance" (2 Peter 3:9). So, before anything else is said, God is telling us it is His will that we turn from our sin and put our faith in Jesus Christ as Savior and Lord. I know that's a "no-brainer" but we need to start there.

Here's another.

#2: You need to be filled with and controlled by the Holy Spirit.

Scripture tells us, "Be very careful, then, how you live—not as unwise but as wise, making the most of every opportunity, because the days are evil. Therefore do not be foolish, but understand what the Lord's will is. Do not get drunk on wine, which leads to debauchery. Instead, be filled with the Spirit. Speak to one another with psalms, hymns and spiritual songs. Sing and make music in your heart to the Lord, always giving thanks to God the Father for everything, in the name of our Lord Jesus Christ" (Ephesians 5:15–20, NIV).

Take a close look at the phrase *"be filled."* In the original language this term appears in the present tense. In other words, "*constantly* be filled." It is also a command. It is the unmistakable will of God that every believer be continually filled with His Spirit.

So God is saying, "It is My will, My very command to you, My child, that you be constantly filled with My Holy Spirit."

Are you being obedient to the clear command of the Lord? Are you opening your heart to the filling and leading of His Spirit? By the way, to be "filled with the Spirit" has little or nothing to do with your emotions. That word *filled* comes from a word that means "controlled."

God wants you to yield to the leading of His Holy Spirit each and every day.

#3: You need to live a pure life.

"For this is the will of God, even your sanctification that is, that you abstain from sexual immorality" (1 Thessalonians 4:3).

How's that for clear and direct?

The word *sanctification* means holiness, consecration, and dedication to God. This speaks to single people to remain sexually pure until marriage and faithful to one's spouse after. There are no exceptions to this rule of Scripture. God will not lead you to do something His Word clearly forbids. Period.

I bring this up because I have actually had unmarried couples tell me that the Lord told them is was okay for them to sleep together. This is clearly not the case, as evidenced by this and many other passages of Scripture.

#4: You need an attitude of gratitude.

"In everything give thanks, for this is the will of God in Christ Jesus concerning you" (1 Thessalonians 5:18).

Do you see it? *"This is the will of God… concerning you."* There's nothing vague or foggy about that, is there?

This is simply an attitude that recognizes that God is in control of all circumstances that surround your life. He leads us to both still waters and stormy seas. It's all a part of the process of making us more like Jesus. He wants you to give thanks to Him as a discipline of your life.

JUST ASK

Now, having received some specific biblical guidelines for your life, there is absolutely nothing wrong with asking the Lord for personal direction as well. The apostle James tells us, "If you need wisdom—if you want to know what God wants you to do—ask him, and he will gladly tell you. He will not resent your asking. But when you ask him, be sure that you really expect him to answer, for a doubtful mind is as unsettled as a wave of the sea that is driven and tossed by the wind. People like that should not expect to receive anything from the Lord" (James 1:5–8, NLT).

An old Jewish Proverb says, "It is better to ask the way ten times than to take the wrong road once."

We men have a reputation for not being fond of asking for directions. That's probably why the Israelites wandered for forty years when they could have reached their destination in forty days. None of the men wanted to ask for directions!

That was meant as humor, but the fact is God does want us to ask Him for direction in our lives.

He reminds us, "You have not, because you ask not."

PREPARING THE GROUND

Let's look at some steps we can take to prepare the ground to hear the voice of God and know His will.

> I beseech you therefore, brethren, by the
> mercies of God, that you present your
> bodies a living sacrifice, holy, acceptable to
> God, which is your reasonable service. And
> do not be conformed to this world, but be
> transformed by the renewing of your mind,
> that you may prove what is that good and
> acceptable and perfect will of God.
> (Romans 12:1–2)

Notice the order: the "living sacrifice" part first, then discovering the will of God. We tend to want to know His will first—then decide if we want to give ourselves to it or not! It would be like someone saying, "Can you do me a favor?" and we respond "What's that?" We answer that way because we want to find out what it is before we do it. Loan them a buck? No problem. Help them paint their house? No way!

So God says, "Will you do My will?" And we respond, "What is it?" But in essence God says, *"Give Me your life and I will show you My will."* It's when we learn this lesson we are ready for an exciting life of God continually unfolding His will for us!

"Present your bodies a living sacrifice…" (verse 1).

The language here is of an offering, something we do willingly.

God wants the heartfelt gift of our life, time, and resources—not out of duty but out of love. If you don't want to do this you don't have to. On the other hand you miss out on all the benefits of complete surrender to Jesus Christ, including His revealed will in your life.

The condition of an enlightened mind is a surrendered heart.

"Be not conformed to this world…"

This world system is spiritually bankrupt and hostile to God. John writes: "Stop loving this evil world and all that it offers you, for when you love the world, you show that you do not have the love of the Father in you. For the world offers only the lust for physical pleasure, the lust for everything we see, and pride in our possessions. These are not from the Father. They are from this evil world. And this world is fading away, along with everything it craves. But if you do the will of God, you will live forever" (1 John 2:15–17).

The Greek verb *conform* refers to the act of assuming an outward appearance that does not accurately reflect what is within. In other words,

Paul is saying, "Don't masquerade as if you belong to the world; that would be patterning yourself inconsistently with who you really are!" Or as the Phillips translation renders it, "Don't let the world squeeze you into its mold."

And The Greg Translation? "Don't be a wannabe." You are a child of God. Don't hide it, be proud of it!

In this day when it is acceptable and in style to openly mock and deride Christians, we may find ourselves tempted to mask our Christianity, or to be ashamed that we belong to Jesus. In 2 Timothy 2:12, Paul writes: "If we endure, we will also reign with him. If we disown him, he will also disown us."

We as believers should never be ashamed of the Gospel of Christ. Jesus said, "If anyone is ashamed of Me and My words in this adulterous and sinful generation, the Son of Man will be ashamed of him when He comes in His Father's glory with the holy angels" (Mark 8:38).

Paul said, "I am not ashamed of the gospel of Christ" (Romans 1:16).

If you've grown up in the church, you've heard that declaration a thousand times. It might be easy to pass it off with a shrug. Just remember, that very same Gospel cost Paul everything—his comfort, his health, his reputation, his career, his freedom, and ultimately his life.

You and I, however, may find ourselves under constant pressure to downplay our convictions. Sometimes we find it difficult to discern God's will because we've become so immersed in a way of thinking that is quite worldly—a secular mind set. This is the kind of thinking that would eliminate God and His Word from the decision-making process. It would be a person who would reason primarily from his or her own selfish point of view—a "me first" world view, instead of considering God first. For instance, if you are having problems in your marriage or become enamored with someone else, you may well think to yourself, *"Well, I'll just get a divorce."* And worse than that, some will even dare to suggest, *"The Lord led me…."*

Instead of being conformed, we must be *transformed* from this world's warped and selfish way of thinking. The word is literally, *transfigured*. Quite frankly we need to be brainwashed. I don't mean that, of course, in the common way that term is used. I mean that our brains, our minds, our way of thinking need to be cleansed from this secular, worldly outlook. This will happen as we spend time in fellowship with God and His people. When we saturate our lives and thoughts with the Word of God, then (and only then) will we begin to grasp God's will for our lives.

As I reject conformity to this world system and its self-indulgent ways, allowing myself instead to be molded into the image of Jesus, His purpose for my life will unfold panel by panel, like a road map.

It's really a process of elimination. Eliminate all those influences that would cloud your way of thinking. You might think of it like tuning in to the right frequency on a radio dial, tuning out other signals that would distract.

Someone once asked a concert violinist in New York's Carnegie Hall how she became so skilled. She replied, "By planned neglect." In other words, she planned to neglect everything that was not related to her goal.

"...The good and acceptable and perfect will of God." (verse 2)

First of all, we need to realize God's will for us is good! David wrote, "O taste and see that the

Lord is good: blessed is the man that trusts in Him"
(Psalm 34:8).

Many of us have a warped concept of God as
being some kind of "Celestial Party-Pooper," who is
just waiting for you to surrender your will to His so
He can make you miserable!

Nothing could be further from the truth! Think
back to our Lord's story of the prodigal son. When
this wandering young man finally found his way
home, what was his father's first response after the
warm welcome? "Let's throw a party!"

God's will is not only good, it also is perfect. No
plan of ours can improve on the plan of God. We
only see bits and pieces; He sees the whole. We see
only fragments of the past—and nothing at all of
the future. God says, "I know the thoughts I think
toward you…thoughts of peace and not of evil,
to give you a future and a hope" (or, literally, "an
expected end") (Jeremiah 29:11).

You may not know this, but I am an artist.
Sometimes I'll be working on a drawing, and
someone will come up, look over my shoulder, and
say, "What's that? It just looks like a circle." Well,
maybe they see a circle. But I see what I'm going to
put *in* the circle.

As they are breathing down my neck, I will say, "Would you just wait until I'm done?" In the same way, we may find ourselves breathing over God's shoulder, waiting for things to happen in our life, waiting for our future to take shape. And God essentially says to us, "It's not done yet, so will you just wait until I'm done?"

God is still finishing you. Or maybe He's just getting started! You are a work in progress. So don't be impatient. Don't throw in the towel just because you're not where you want to be yet. We see only the beginning. God sees "the expected end," and it's good! Ecclesiastes 3:11 says, "God has made everything beautiful for its own time. He has planted eternity in the human heart, but even so, people cannot see the whole scope of God's work from beginning to end."

Don't be afraid to completely surrender to the will of God for your lives. Don't be afraid to say, "Not my will but Yours be done…" Never be afraid to commit an unknown future to a known God. I may not know what the future holds, but I know who holds the future.

SO HOW DOES GOD SPEAK?

#1: First and foremost, He speaks through His Word.

"Your word is a lamp unto my feet and a light unto my path" (Psalm 119:105).

He will never, never lead us contrary to the written Word. It is our litmus test, our bedrock, our absolute. The Bible is the clear revelation by which we measure all other so-called "revelations." It is the rock of stability with which we measure our fickle human emotions. The way we know something is true or right is by comparing it to what Scripture teaches. The book of Acts tells us that the believers in Berea "searched [or 'scrutinized'] the scriptures to see if these things were true" (cf. Acts 17:11).

Everything you need to know about God is found in the pages of Scripture. Paul wrote to young Timothy, "All Scripture is inspired by God and is useful to teach us what is true and to make us realize what is wrong in our lives. It straightens us out and teaches us to do what is right. It is God's way of preparing us in every way, fully equipped for every good thing God wants us to do" (2 Timothy 3:16, NLT).

From this Scripture, then, we know that God

would never lead us contrary to what the Bible plainly teaches. This seems so obvious (and it is), but it's amazing how many seem to miss the point. They're busy seeking some "mystical" word from God, when He has already plainly spoken to them in the pages of Scripture.

It would be like desperately longing to hear from someone that you deeply loved. Then one day you looked in your mailbox and found a letter from them, or an e-mail from them on your computer. But imagine that instead of opening the letter, you continued to whine about how this person never communicates with you.

Open the letter!

In the same way, we must open the Book!

Jesus said, "Behold, I have come; in the volume of the book it is written of Me; to do Your will, O God" (Hebrews 10:7). That doesn't mean you hold your Bible up to the wind in some random, superstitious way, and say… "Speak to me, O God!" We need to read the Bible chapter by chapter, verse by verse, getting the "whole counsel of God."

Why do we do this? Because there is always the danger of misinterpreting the Word or wrenching it out of its proper context. This is what the devil did with Jesus during the temptation in the wilderness.

> The devil led him to Jerusalem and had him
> stand on the highest point of the temple.
> "If you are the Son of God," he said, "throw
> yourself down from here. For it is written:
> 'He will command his angels concerning
> you to guard you carefully; they will lift you
> up in their hands, so that you will not strike
> your foot against a stone.'" (Luke 4:9–11)

But the devil left something out.

He was quoting from Psalm 91:11–12. But
Jesus brought it back into context, saying, "It
is written, 'You shall not tempt the Lord your
God.'" Remember this. Scripture will never, ever
contradict itself. That means that if you find some
text and build an entire case on it, yet it doesn't
coincide with the rest of Scripture, it is wrong. I've
had guys and girls tell me that God led them to
date an unbeliever. But what do you do with
2 Corinthians 6:14?

> "Do not be unequally yoked together with
> unbelievers. For what fellowship has righteousness
> with lawlessness? And what communion has light
> with darkness?"

No matter what your emotions or hormones

may be demanding of you, violating God's Word will never take you down the right path. In fact, you will find yourself in great peril.

#2: God speaks to us through circumstances.

There are times and situations in our lives where we ask God to confirm His Word to us. Gideon did this. God had told him that he was to lead the people into battle against a huge force of invaders. But Gideon was no soldier, and he had to ask the Lord if he'd really heard Him right! He said, "Lord, if You have told me to do this, I'm putting a fleece on the ground in the morning. If there's dew on the fleece but the ground is dry, I will then know this was You speaking to me." And it happened just as he asked.

Still lacking confidence over this huge and deadly task, Gideon reversed his request, asking that it be dry on the ground but wet on the fleece (Judges 6:36–40). This is not the best way to determine God's will, but it does make a point.

If the Lord is in it He will confirm it.

In the book of Acts, God told Philip to go to the desert. There was no itinerary, no GPS coordinates, no detailed plans or blueprints. In fact, no reason was given at all. It was just the bare command, "Go to the desert."

Philip obeyed. And when he got there, it was confirmed.

Paul was stopped on his journey at certain points by shipwreck, sickness, and a long jail term.

God speaks to His people through occurrences like these, as the Bible records countless times.

#3: Lastly, there is that work in your heart.

It may be a spiritual stirring deep within you. You sense something happening. You feel the need to spend more time in prayer, perhaps fasting, and seeking God's face. And when you begin to move by His leading, you will experience His peace. Scripture says, "Let the peace of Christ rule in your hearts, since as members of one body you were called to peace. And be thankful" (Colossians 3:15, NIV). A literal rendering of that verse reads, "Let the peace of God as an umpire settle with all finality all matters that arise in your hearts."

I might add there is also the issue of God's timing.

Moses, for instance, had the right idea as a young man, when he struck down an Egyptian in order to save one of his countrymen. But his timing was a bit off. By about forty years!

> *If the request is wrong, God says, "No."*
> *If the timing is wrong, God says, "Slow."*
> *If you are wrong, God says, "Grow."*
> *But if the request is right, the timing is right,* and you are right, God says, "Go!"

A FINAL WORD

Let me come back to something I said in the beginning of this chapter. God's will for you first and foremost is that you be saved. Scripture says that "God is not willing that any should perish, but that all should come to repentance" (2 Peter 3:9). Amazing as it may be to think about, God wants to enter into friendship with you.

He wants to reveal His secrets to you.

He wants to make Himself known to you.

He has a unique and custom-made plan just for you!

You are not a mere statistic or blip on some cosmic radar screen.

You are not a result of some random evolutionary process. You are a person made in the very image of God Himself. And He is calling you to Himself right now!

There is no sweeter place on the whole planet than smack-dab in the center of God's will for you.

What the Devil Doesn't Want **You to Know**

The day you asked Jesus Christ to come into your life, forgive your sins, and be your Savior and Lord was the greatest day of your life.

Nothing in all of life—not the day of your graduation, not the day of your marriage, not the birth of your first child—can compare with *that* day.

It was the day your destiny changed for eternity.

It was the day you passed from darkness to light.

It was the day you found purpose and meaning beyond what you had ever experienced before.

The Bible tells us that there is "rejoicing in heaven" when one sinner comes to Jesus Christ. Interpret that however you will. Angels doing back-flips? A song of joy breaking out across the spiritual universe? The believers who have gone before you cheering from the grandstands?

I'm not sure what shape that rejoicing might take. But I know it is real, because God says that it is.

But there is another dynamic you need to know about. There is another side to what happened on that day when you said "yes" to Jesus. And though that "something" doesn't have to steal your confidence or your joy, it ought to move you to keep your eyes open and your guard up as you walk through this life.

Because the day of your salvation was the day the real *spiritual war* in your life began.

THE WAR BEGINS

Becoming a Christian, the best decision you ever made, doesn't mean that you'll be walking along sunlit paths through California poppies for the rest of your life.

In fact, that decision launches a war that will follow you all your days until Jesus takes you to His Father's house. "Conversion," someone wrote, "has made our hearts a battlefield."

Just as you came to realize that there is a God who loves you, you also must come to understand that there is a devil who hates you.

And that devil wants to pull you right back
into sin—right back into the snares and traps and
sorrows of the old life from which you just escaped.
In one of the stories Jesus told, sometimes called
"the parable of the sower," He spoke about what
happens right after the living seed of God's Word is
planted in someone's heart. "And these are the ones
by the wayside where the word is sown. When they
hear, Satan comes immediately and takes away the
word that was sown in their hearts" (Mark 4:15).

If the evil one fails in that task, he will simply
battle with you, contending each forward step
you take for Jesus Christ. The devil's "ultimate
objective," as the Lord tells us in John 10:10, is to
"to steal, and to kill, and to destroy." So until the
day we finally walk through the doorway of heaven,
the spiritual warfare will rage on.

The believer may be known by his inward
warfare as well as by his inward peace. This battle
is not against flesh and blood. *It is spiritual battle!*
With a very real devil. As Martin Luther wrote in
the classic hymn:

> For still our ancient foe
> Doth seek to work us woe.

> His craft and power are great,
> and armed with cruel hate
> On earth is not his equal.

We should never underestimate the devil. He is a sly and skillful adversary, with thousands of years of experience dealing with mankind. But even though he is a wily and powerful foe, he also has clear weaknesses, and can be overcome.

THE ORIGIN OF SATAN

Through the course of my ministry, I've often been asked, "Why would God create someone as horrible as Satan?"

The answer is that God did not create Satan—at least, not as we know him today. He was once a powerful and high-ranking angel known as Lucifer. But at some point in this mighty angel's career, something went wrong. The thought entered his head that he didn't simply want to worship God, he wanted to *be* a god, he wanted to be worshiped in all his God-given beauty and power. So he rebelled against the God of heaven, and swept one third of the angels along with him in that rebellion.

The Bible gives this being many names, including Satan, the devil, Lucifer, Beelzebub, the father of lies, the god of this world, and the prince of the power of the air. He usually comes in all his depravity, pulling people into vile and sinful directions. *But sometimes he will come as an angel of light, deceiving the untaught and the unwary* (2 Corinthians 11:14).

Recently, I read about some birds in Denmark that are imitating the sound of cell phones. Believe it or not, they have even more cell phones per capita over there than they do in Los Angeles. According to this news article, many of the birds in the city have changed the way they sing, now frequently imitating the sound of a ringing cell phone. One man said he has a bird in his garden that he has named "Nokia." And just like those birds pretending to be cell phones, Satan will approach us appearing to be something he is not, seeking to deceive us.

If we want to effectively resist him, we need to understand his "M.O."—his method of operation. The Bible says, "Resist the devil and he will flee from you" (James 4:7).

But how do you do that? How do you stand against a being who burns with hate for God and people, leads an army of countless demons, and who has been seeking to destroy men and women since the beginning of time?

First by knowing about his strategies and weaknesses. *And there are many.* Let me start by sharing a few things the devil does not want you to know.

SATAN IS NOT THE EQUAL OF GOD

It isn't even close!

God is *omnipotent.* He is unlimited in power and might. Satan is not. Yes, he has great power—more than any man and most angels. Yet he is nowhere near being the equal of our God.

God is *omniscient.* He knows everything there is to know down to the tiniest, atom-sized details. Satan does not. Our adversary is not omniscient. He has a powerful intellect, a long memory, and from experience knows many things—far more than people. But only God is all-knowing.

God is *omnipresent.* There is nowhere that He is not! He is everywhere at once all the time. Satan is limited. As an individual personality, he can only be in one place at one time. So when we say "the devil is hassling or tempting me," it's not likely. It is his power working through a well organized network of demonic forces.

But there is another thing the devil doesn't want you to know.

HE IS SUBJECT TO GOD'S PERMISSION

The evil one can do nothing in the life of a believer without permission from God. The book of Job gives an account of the angels presenting themselves before God—an amazing "behind the scenes" look at what happens in the spiritual realm.

> One day the angels came to present themselves before the LORD, and Satan the Accuser came with them. "Where have you come from?" the LORD asked Satan.

> And Satan answered the LORD, "I have been going back and forth across the earth, watching everything that's going on."

> Then the LORD asked Satan, "Have you noticed my servant Job? He is the finest man in all the earth—a man of complete integrity. He fears God and will have nothing to do with evil."

Satan replied to the LORD, "Yes, Job fears God, but not without good reason! You have always protected him and his home and his property from harm. You have made him prosperous in everything he does. Look how rich he is!" (Job 1:6–10, NLT)

A number of truths strike us from this text.

First of all, we see that Satan, even after his fall, still has access to the throne of God. He has lost his once high-ranking position, but he still has access.

Second, we see that in spite of his power and wicked agenda, he has to *ask permission* when it comes to the child of God, because of this "hedge of protection" God has put in place. In one instance in the gospel of John, it appears that Satan himself was specifically asking for Simon Peter by name. Jesus said to Peter: "Simon, Simon, behold, Satan has demanded permission to sift you like wheat; but I have prayed for you, that your faith may not fail; and you, when once you have turned again, strengthen your brothers" (Luke 22:31–32, NASB).

Apparently, Peter was such a "big fish" that Satan himself went knocking. Thankfully, God knows our breaking point, and won't give us more than we can handle. That's a promise!

No temptation has overtaken you except
such as is common to man; but God is
faithful, who will not allow you to be
tempted beyond what you are able, but with
the temptation will also make the way of
escape, that you may be able to bear it.
(1 Corinthians 10:13)

Now, this is not to say that you cannot put
yourself in a place of temptation—a place where
you don't belong. King David ought to have been
leading the armies of Israel in its battles, but he
stayed home instead. And with idle time on his
hands, strolling on his rooftop one evening, he saw
what he should have never seen, and did what he
should never have done (see 2 Samuel 11).

Jesus taught us to pray, "And do not lead us
into temptation, but deliver us from the evil one."
We cannot completely remove ourselves from
temptation. To do that, we'd have to leave the
planet. In this petition we are asking God to so
guide our steps that we will not wander out of His
will and place ourselves in the way of temptation.
We're saying, "Lord, don't let me be tempted above
my capacity to resist."

I heard the story of a guy who was quite

overweight and wanted to shed some pounds. Knowing his propensity for eating donuts, he even changed his normal route he took to drive to work so as to avoid driving by Krispy Kreme® donuts. He did this successfully for three weeks and all his coworkers were really proud of him. Then one day he came to work with five boxes of hot Krispy Kremes—three of them already consumed.

Everyone started getting on his case for falling off the wagon. He smiled and said, "Wait, these are special donuts! I accidentally drove by Krispy Kreme in the morning, and I could see the sign was lit up telling me the donuts were being made fresh.

"So I prayed, 'Lord, if You want me to have some of these incredible donuts, let me have a parking space right in front of the store!' And sure enough, the eighth time around the block, there it was!"

That reminds me of a bumper sticker: "Lead me not into temptation. I can find it myself."

It's important for us to know that Satan does not work alone. He has help from his massive demon army doing his bidding. Let's learn a bit more about them.

THE EVIL ARMY

Finally, my brethren, be strong in the Lord
and in the power of His might. Put on the
whole armor of God, that you may be able
to stand against the wiles of the devil. For
we do not wrestle against flesh and blood,
but against principalities, against powers,
against the rulers of the darkness of this
age, against spiritual hosts of wickedness in
the heavenly places. Therefore take up the
whole armor of God, that you may be able to
withstand in the evil day, and having done
all, to stand. (Ephesians 6:10–13)

When Paul uses the words *"We wrestle not...,"*
it's a term describing life and death hand-to-hand
combat. As I said, the day we believed a very real
spiritual conflict began in our lives. The devil
directs a well-organized, highly effective army
of fallen angels to do his work. And all his work is
"dirty work."

Verse twelve tells us that we wrestle against
*"principalities, against powers, against the rulers
of the darkness of this age, against spiritual hosts
of wickedness in the heavenly places."*

We read numerous passages that refer to Satan

and his minions:

- *"Beelzebub, the prince of the demons…."*
  (Matthew 12:24)

- *"The devil and his angels…." (Matthew 25:41)*

- *"The dragon…and his angels…."*
  (Revelation 12:7, 9)

And of course, hell is the future dwelling-place "for the devil and his angels."

The purpose of demons seems to be twofold. They seek to hinder the purposes of God and to extend the power of Satan. We see this illustrated in Scripture. Consider this snippet from Paul's letter to the church in Thessalonica: "For we wanted to come to you—certainly I, Paul, did, again and again—but Satan stopped us" (1 Thessalonians 2:18).

Paul mentioned his own personal struggles that were brought on by demons, and allowed by God. Because of the great blessings and revelations that God had brought into his life, considerable hardship and suffering were allowed in his life as well.

In his second letter to the Corinthians, he reveals this highly personal account of his struggles: "And lest I should be exalted above measure by the abundance of the revelations, a thorn in the flesh was given to me, a messenger of Satan to buffet me, lest I be exalted above measure. Concerning this thing I pleaded with the Lord three times that it might depart from me. And He said to me, 'My grace is sufficient for you, for My strength is made perfect in weakness.' Therefore most gladly I will rather boast in my infirmities, that the power of Christ may rest upon me" (2 Corinthians 12:7–9).

The word *buffet* in this passage means to "rap," or to "strike with the fist." Though it's true we as believers can be hassled like Paul was, and tempted and oppressed and harassed by Satan, *the devil cannot control us!* The apostle said, "We get knocked down, but we get up again and keep going" (2 Corinthians 4:9, NLT).

Though the nonbeliever is essentially a sitting duck for full-blown demon possession, the true believer need not fear. *Every move of the enemy must come by permission through the protective hedge of Jesus.*

Someone may ask, "Greg, are you telling me you actually believe in demon possession?" *Absolutely!* In the New Testament we see people who were possessed by demons having many illnesses as well as suicidal tendencies.

There was one man who was possessed by not one but many, many demons. He hung around in a graveyard, naked, cutting himself with sharp rocks. He had super-human strength, and was able to break chains with his bare hands. No doubt the people of the area avoided this place—especially at night. Superstitious people would have said this was a place for ghosts and goblins!

Nobody would set foot in this place…except Jesus.

The Amplified Bible says of this man, "Night and day among the tombs and on the mountains he was always shrieking and screaming and beating and bruising and cutting himself with stones" (Mark 5:5).

How Satan and his dark angels hate human beings! And this was a man who was completely given over to Satan. How does this happen?

By opening the door to your soul.

Again, this is something the nonbeliever can do, not the Christian.

There are many that open the door to the supernatural through drugs. There is a definite link between drugs and the occult. The Bible warns of the sin of sorcery. The word *sorcery* comes from the Greek word *pharmakia*, from which we get our English word *pharmacy*.

The biblical definition of *sorcery* has to do with the illicit use of drugs. When people begin to use drugs, whether it's marijuana, LSD, ecstasy, or any other mind-controlling substances, it opens them up to the spiritual realm. Dabbling in black magic, witchcraft, Ouija boards or astrology can also open the door.

Note that the man was suicidal. When I look at the rash of suicides in our country today, especially among young people, I have to say Satan is at work. I recently read a tragic story of a young man who killed himself just two years after his brother did the same thing.

Suicides among adolescents have nearly tripled over the last forty years. For those ages fifteen to twenty-four, suicide is the third leading cause of death, behind accidents and homicide.

The devil whispers in your ear, *"You are worthless, take your life!"*

Remember, his ultimate agenda is to "steal, to kill, and to destroy." Jesus transformed this tortured man, releasing him from an army of evil spirits in the space of a heartbeat.

This is a reminder to us that when Christ comes in, the devil goes out. And that's why it's wrong when we hear people saying Christians can be "demon-possessed." Believers might allow themselves to be hassled, harassed, or hounded by demons, but those evil angels cannot enter a space occupied by the living Christ! God is not interested in a time-share program with the devil.

COUNTER HIS STRATEGIES

Personally, I want to keep as much distance between the devil and myself as possible. We need to flee temptation—and not leave a forwarding address! Why? Because flirtation with sin can lead to romance with Satan. For this reason, we must be very, very careful not to yield to him. The Bible says we don't have to be ignorant of his devices… in other words, his strategies and deceits (2 Corinthians 2:11).

There are so many "reality TV" programs on the air these days, it's hard to remember where the whole craze started. If I remember correctly, it was "Survivor," and the program was all about strategy.

In the first "Survivor" series, the wily Richard played the game and won a million dollars.

The devil has strategy, too. He sizes you up, looking for weaknesses and vulnerabilities. First he attacks through the obvious temptations: drugs, sex, drinking, and so on.

I read an article from *Entertainment Weekly* about drug abuse in Hollywood, called, "Hollywood High." It talked about all the stars who have been in and out of rehab. Some died from overdoses, like Elvis Presley, Kurt Cobain, Jimi Hendrix, Janis Joplin, John Belushi, and Chris Farley.

This problem has become so bad that many Hollywood sets offer on-site drug counseling. What's interesting to me, is that many of these celebrities have their worst problems when they are at the top of their game. One well-known screenwriter said, "I've known hundreds of people who have been addicts. They all share one thing. They feel a huge emptiness they thought could be filled with some finite substance—drugs, booze, women."

Satan would love to snag you into addiction. Better yet (in his book), kill you off early. He would like to chew you up and spit you out.

Now let's look at something else the devil doesn't want you to know.

ACCUSING YOU BEFORE GOD

One of his most effective strategies is to pull you down through temptation, and then accuse you before the throne of God. On more than one occasion he is referred to as an *accuser!*

> Now salvation, and strength, and the kingdom of our God, and the power of His Christ have come, *for the accuser of our brethren, who accused them before our God day and night, has been cast down.* (Revelation 12:10)

Back in the story of Job I mentioned earlier, Satan says to God (with a sneer), "Does Job fear you for nothing? …All that a man has he will give for his life!" (Job 1:9, 2:4).

You would think that Satan, having led the person into sin, would then leave him to suffer the consequences; but this is not what happens. He wants to make the disobedient Christian doubly defeated. It's his "double whammy"!

When you and I have disobeyed God, Satan moves in for that finishing stroke. Satan still uses this tactic with great effect! "You call yourself a Christian? Do you think a holy God will hear *your* prayer! Ha! After what *you* did?"

See how subtle he is? Before we sin, while he is tempting us, he whispers, *"You can get away with this..."* After we sin he shouts, *"You will never get away with this..."*

It is very, very important that we learn to distinguish between Satan's accusation and the Spirit's conviction. A feeling of guilt and shame isn't necessarily a bad thing if it comes from the Spirit of God. But if it drives us to despair and hopelessness, we've listened to the *wrong voice*.

When the Spirit of God convicts you, He uses the Word of God in love and seeks to bring you back into fellowship with your heavenly Father. When Satan accuses you he uses your own sins in a hateful way, and seeks to make you feel helpless and hopeless.

Remember his End Game. *"To steal, to kill, and to destroy"!* Satan wants you to feel guilty and condemned. He wants you to experience regret and remorse—but not repentance. He wants to keep accusing you so that you focus your attention on yourself and your sins...and let your eyes slip away from the Lord who loves you and redeems you. In contrast, true conviction from the Spirit will move you closer to the Lord.

Judas listened to the devil and went out and hanged himself in complete despair. Peter looked at the face of Jesus and wept bitterly, but later came back into fellowship with Christ.

Remember this simple truth. Satan will always seek to drive you away from the Cross. God's Spirit will always you draw you to it. Don't let "hell or high-water" keep you from coming to the Cross, repenting of your sin, and experiencing the wonderful, cleansing work of forgiveness in your life!

Yes, you can expect the evil one to say to you, "You're not worthy to approach God! Not after what you've done!"

This is such an old, worn tool out of his toolbox that you'd think he'd get tired of using it. But why should he? It works! It has worked for millennia. And as long as it keeps doing the job he wants done in a life, he'll keep right on using it.

Sometimes you may find that the "father of

lies" uses a bit of truth—just to make his lies more credible. In fact, it was his very first strategy, back in the Garden of Eden with Eve. He took just a few of God's words, twisted them, and mixed them with his own. And Eve fell through deception.

When he tried the same thing with Jesus Himself in the wilderness, quoting a bit of Scripture out of context, his strategy hit a brick wall. The Author of Scripture wasn't going to be fooled by someone twisting His own words!

Do you see how important it is for you and I to be reading God's Word every day, seeking God's face, and walking in the fullness of His Holy Spirit? We need the Spirit's help to identify and filter out Satan's lies from God's truth.

Remember, Jesus said to Peter, "Satan has been asking for you…but I have prayed for you." Our defense against the accusations of the devil is the Son of God, who intercedes and prays for us before the Father.

> My little children, these things I write to you, so that you may not sin. And if anyone sins, we have an Advocate with the Father, Jesus Christ the righteous. (1 John 2:1)

Who will bring any charge against those

whom God has chosen? It is God who justifies. Who is he that condemns? Christ Jesus, who died—more than that, who was raised to life—is at the right hand of God and is also interceding for us. (Romans 8:33)

Let me tell you one final thing the devil does not want you to know.

HE WAS SOUNDLY DEFEATED AT THE CROSS OF CALVARY

Prior to His crucifixion on the cross, Jesus said, "Now is the judgment of this world: now shall the prince of this world be cast out" (John 12:31). Referring to this same event on Calvary, Jesus said, "The prince of this world is judged" (John 16:11).

Through His death on the cross Jesus destroyed *"him that had the power of death, that is, the devil"* (Hebrews 2:14).

On the cross, just before He yielded up His spirit, Jesus cried out the words *"It is finished!"* or *"It is accomplished!"* What was accomplished? The work the Father had given Him to do. And what was finished was Satan's death grip on humanity.

Colossians 2:13–14 says: "When you were dead in your transgressions…He made you alive together with Him, having forgiven us all our transgressions, having canceled out the certificate of debt consisting of decrees against us, which was hostile to us; and He has taken it out of the way, having nailed it to the cross."

So we fight and engage in spiritual warfare, yes. But we are not fighting to *obtain* victory. (Oh, how the devil hates you to hear this!) We are resting *in* the victory our Lord Jesus has already obtained! We don't fight FOR victory *("Oh Lord, give me victory in this!");* we fight FROM victory *("Lord, I thank You that You won't give me more than I can handle!").*

But once again, I must emphasize that these liberating truths only apply to those who belong to Jesus Christ. If you have not yet asked Jesus to come into your life, you are a "sitting duck," defenseless against the fierce enemy of your soul.

Paul speaks of those outside of Christ, urging his young disciple to teach the truth so that "they will come to their senses and escape from the devil's trap. For they have been held captive by him to do whatever he wants" (2 Timothy 2:26, NLT).

Back in the very first days of His ministry, the Lord Jesus declared why He had come and what He was all about. Quoting from the prophet Isaiah, He said, "The Spirit of the LORD is upon Me, because He has anointed Me to preach the gospel to the poor; He has sent Me to heal the brokenhearted, to proclaim liberty to the captives and recovery of sight to the blind, to set at liberty those who are oppressed" (Luke 4:18).

Satan would like nothing better than to break the hearts of men and women, take them captive, blind them to beauty and truth and hope, and lock them up in chains of addiction and oppression.

But that's why Jesus came. He brings Good News of salvation, hope, release, and a fresh, clean life. He spreads His balm of healing over broken hearts, tortured minds, and bruised souls. He touches the eyes of those who have been spiritually blind, so that they can see the truth and find the path of life. And He opens the prison doors, allowing those who have been held captive by Satan for most of their lives to walk free, out into the sunshine and fresh wind of His love.

Satan doesn't want you to know any of those things.

But now you do.

The Need for
Godly Fathers

Godly dads are the unsung heroes of our country today.

Greater than any athlete, rock star, or celebrity.

More influential than any politician.

We don't give enough credit to fathers these days.

Mark Twain wrote, "When I was a boy of fourteen, my father was so ignorant I could hardly stand to have the old man around. But when I got to be twenty-one, I was astonished at how much he had learned in seven years!"

I'm reminded of a clipping from a Dutch magazine I read a number of years ago.

> At 4 years old, the child says: "My daddy can do anything."

At 7 years old, he says, "My daddy knows a whole lot."

At 8 years, "Dad doesn't know quite everything."

At 12 years, "Oh, well, naturally my dad doesn't know that, either."

At 14 years, "Dad is hopelessly old-fashioned."

At 21 years, "He is so out-of-date!"

At 25 years, "He knows a little bit about it, but not too much."

At 30 years, "I need to find out what Dad thinks about it."

At 35 years, "Before we decide, we need to get Dad's idea first."

At 50 years, "What would Dad have thought about that?"

At 60 years, "My dad knew literally everything."

At 65 years, "I wish I could talk it over with

Dad one more time."

How important good and godly dads are—more than ever! The father that faithfully stands by his wife and children through all the highs and lows of life is becoming more and more of a rarity in our culture. I don't want to come off as overdramatic, but our country needs you! We've all heard the Marine Corps slogan, "Looking for a few good men." The new slogan of our country ought to be, "Looking for a few godly men."

FOR THE LACK OF A FATHER

It's an established fact that most of our social ills today can be directly traced to the lack of fathers in our homes. In an article from the L.A. *Times Magazine*, entitled, "The Invisible Dad," the writer pointed out that "many American men are disconnecting from family life, and society is paying the price."

Consider two of our nation's most serious problems—crime and teenage pregnancy. Studies show that the most reliable predictor of these behaviors is not income, nor race. It is family structure. Pregnant girls and criminal boys tend to come from fatherless families. An astonishing seventy percent of imprisoned U.S. minors have spent at least part of their lives living without fathers.

Father Greg Boyle of Dolores Mission Church in East Los Angeles once listed the names of the first one hundred gang members that came to mind, and then jotted a family history next to each. All but five were no longer living with their biological fathers—*if they ever had*. Without men around as role models, adolescent boys create their own rites of passage: perhaps getting a girl pregnant, or dealing drugs, or murdering a rival.

Throughout history, men have been torn from their families by war, difficult jobs in faraway places, disease, and death.

But in 21st century America, men are simply walking away.

They are choosing to disconnect from family life on a massive scale—and at far higher rates than other industrialized countries. Men are drifting away from family life…and we are in danger of becoming a fatherless society.

Why is this a particularly difficult problem in America? I think you can trace it to the same root that's causing so many American marriages to fail.

In a word, it is *selfishness*. When the road of life gets a little bumpy, a little steep, instead of shifting into four-wheel drive and powering up that hill, men are slipping into reverse and backing away from the challenge.

When marriage and raising kids gets tough, many men are saying, "I'm no longer fulfilled in this marriage. Aren't I supposed to be happy?" Or if a younger, more attractive woman than their precious wife comes along, they bail.

Many men abandon wife and children after an affair. Whenever I hear a husband (or wife) say, "We've fallen out of love," or "There's no one else. I just don't love her (him) anymore"…in almost every case there *is* someone else. He or she just isn't telling you.

I read the story of a man who wrote to Ann Landers:

Dear Ann Landers:

Ten years ago I left my wife and four teenagers to marry my secretary, with whom I'd been having an affair. I felt I couldn't live without her. When my wife found out about us, she went to pieces. We were divorced. My wife went to work and did a good job educating the boys. I gave her the house and part of my retirement fund.

I am fairly happy in my second marriage, but I'm beginning to see things in a different light. It hit me when I was a guest at my oldest son's wedding. That's all I was—a guest. I am no longer considered part of the family. My first wife knew everyone present and they showered her with affection. She remarried, and her husband has been taken inside the circle that was once ours. They gave the rehearsal dinner and I sat next to my sons and their sweethearts. I was proud to have a young, pretty wife at my side. But it didn't make up for the pain when I realized my children no longer love me. They treated me with courtesy, but there was no affection or real caring.

I am going to try to build some bridges, but the prospects don't look promising after being out of their lives for ten years. It's going to be difficult reentering now that they have a stepdad they like. I'm writing in the hope that others will consider all the ramifications before they jump.

Just sign me—Second Thoughts in PA.

AN IMMEASURABLE IMPACT

There's something called "the law of sowing and reaping" that we need to remember. That's why, men, you can't consider bailing even for a moment. The Bible says, "Do not be deceived, God is not mocked; for whatever a man sows, that he will also reap. For he who sows to his flesh will of the flesh reap corruption, but he who sows to the Spirit will of the Spirit reap everlasting life" (Galatians 6:7–8).

You need to stand by that commitment you made to your wife on your wedding day, as if your very life depended on it. Nor can you turn your back on your children. To do so would be the same as deserting your post in the face of battle— careless of the lives of the fellow soldiers who depend on you.

Many of us men feel "ill-equipped" to be good fathers. So rather than face what we regard as our inadequacies, we just walk out the door when things get tough. Listen, *it is infinitely better to be an okay-but-learning dad than to be completely absent.*

When my son Christopher was born, I was just twenty-two years old. I remember thinking, *I don't know anything about fathering!* So I began to study Scripture to find out what I could about being a good dad.

Fathers are the visible link children have to their Father in heaven. In many ways, the viewpoint our children develop about God will come from us. I remember when pro basketball star Charles Barkley expressed frustration over being reminded that he was an example for America's youth. "I'm not a role model," he groused. But he couldn't escape it. Whether he wanted that mantle or not, he already had it. Kids all over the country looked up to him and wanted to emulate him. The question is never are we role models? The question is, *what kind* of role models will we be?

The potential impact of a godly father is almost immeasurable. A recent twenty-six-year study came to the conclusion that fathers who spend more time with their young children appear to have an important influence on how compassionate those kids will be as adults. Parental involvement was the single strongest parent-related factor in adult empathy. Psychologist Richard Koestner, of McGill

University in Montreal, said, "Dads who spent the most time alone with kids more than twice a week, giving baths, meals, and basic care, reared the most compassionate adults."

When a father is not involved in his child's life—or, worse, has abandoned his responsibilities—it can only lead to trouble.

Consider these statistics: 70% of juveniles in state-operated institutions come from fatherless homes; 63% of youth suicides are from fatherless homes; 90% of homeless and runaway children are from fatherless homes.

Do you see a pattern here?

One godly father can make an astounding difference—not only in his own immediate family, but for generations to come!

Having lived fifty-three years now, I have been able to see a few generations.

My grandparents' generation.

My parents' generation.

My generation that is still unfolding.

And my children's generation.

You see, the effects of choices that we made decades ago can still come back to shape your life, for better or for worse, depending on what kind of choices they were. The choices of time are binding in eternity.

Contrast two men from the nineteenth century. Max Jukes and Jonathan Edwards.

Max Jukes lived in New York. He did not believe in Christ or in raising his children in the way of the Lord. He refused to take his children to church, even when they asked to go. Jukes has had 1,026 descendants, and of that number:

- 300 were sent to prison for an average term of 13 years;

- 190 were public prostitutes;

- 680 were admitted alcoholics.

His family, thus far, has cost the state in excess of $420,000. They made no contribution to society.

Contrast his life to that of Jonathan Edwards. Edwards was a pastor, a writer, and later, the president of Princeton. He was also a father with eleven children. Of his known male descendants:

- more than 300 became pastors, missionaries, or theological professors

- 120 were professors at various universities

- 110 became attorneys

- 60 were prominent authors

- 30 were judges

- 14 served as presidents of colleges and universities
- 3 served in the U.S. Congress
- 1 became vice-president of the United States.

Edwards was known to study up to 13 hours a day, yet in spite of his busy schedule of writing, teaching, and pastoring, he made it a habit to come home and spend an hour each day with his children. Fathers, today you are leaving a legacy by your life, words, and actions that will not only affect your children, but your grandchildren—and even your great grandchildren.

Charles Spurgeon wrote, "A good character is the best tombstone. Those who loved you and were helped by you will remember you. So carve your name on hearts, and not on marble."

WHAT THE BIBLE SAYS TO FATHERS

And you, fathers, do not provoke your children to wrath, but bring them up in the training and admonition of the Lord. (Ephesians 6:4)

To "provoke to anger" suggests a repeated, ongoing pattern of treatment that gradually builds up a deep-seated anger and resentment that boils over into outward hostility. There are many ways this can be done, and clearly one such way is by showing favoritism.

In the book of Genesis we read how Isaac favored Esau over Jacob, and Rebekah preferred Jacob over Esau. That created a conflict that followed those boys well into their own adult years. Instead of learning his lesson by the way he had been treated, Jacob repeated the same destructive pattern by later favoring Joseph over his brothers. That in turn created a great conflict and jealousy among them, ripping the family apart for decades.

It can be discouraging—even devastating—to compare one of your children to another.

"Why can't you be more like your brother Joshua? He's so much more athletic than you are!"

"Why can't you be as smart as your sister Brittany? She got all 'A's' when she took this class that you are failing in!"

The resentment resulting from such comparisons can be carried well into the adult years, where the boys or girls are constantly trying to "prove" themselves and still win your approval.

Your son or daughter needs to know that you

are always in their court. No matter how well or poorly they achieve in academics, sports, or whatever they attempt in life, they need to know that no matter what you love and support them. Even when the prodigal was in a sinful state, living in a "far country," he still knew his father loved him and would welcome him. Yes, he realized there would be repercussions for his actions, but he never doubted his father would take him back. He knew his dad was "in his corner"…and that paved a way for him to return home.

DON'T SKIMP ON THE PRAISE

Another way to "provoke your children" is by never complimenting them. You need to verbally tell them you love them and that you are proud of them. You need to notice their achievements, no matter how small they might seem, and give them credit for them, while at the same time helping them to see their own potential and to keep striving to do even better. It's a fine balance.

Whether the apostle Paul was ever a married man or father is something the Scriptures don't tell us. But from the way he spoke about a father's priorities, it sounds like he had either had a good father or a good fatherly role model at some point in his life.

> He wrote to the believers at Thessalonica, "For you know that we dealt with each of you as a father deals with his own children, encouraging, comforting and urging you to live lives worthy of God, who calls you into His kingdom and glory."
> (1 Thessalonians 2:11–12)

What does a dad do? He encourages and comforts, but he also points his son or daughter toward higher goals and a higher path—a life worthy of the God who calls us into His kingdom and glory.

You can "over-praise" your child, and not help him or her to reach higher and try harder. But you can also "under-praise," and not give credit where credit is due. At that point, he or she has no reason to even try.

A friend of mine told me about watching his little boy make a creation out of wooden blocks on the living room floor. When the little guy stepped back to look at his work, this dad had the insight to get down on his knees, put a hand on the little guy's shoulder, and say, "Son, that is amazing! What a good job you do! I'm really proud of you."

The small boy gave a contented sigh, looked up at his dad and said softly, "You just make me feel good."

Parents can always find something that a child genuinely does well, and they should mark that positive quality, draw attention to it, and show appreciation for it.

A child needs approval and encouragement for positive accomplishments every bit as much as he needs correction in things that are not. We dads can easily step into that "correction/criticism" role...but totally miss something that has equal importance: positive feedback for the good qualities and attainments.

Paul writes about the negative, "Don't provoke your children to wrath," but he also writes about the positive: "Bring them up in the training and admonition of the Lord." When both elements are in operation, we're talking about the systematic training of children. It is spontaneous, it is natural, and it is constant.

STRONG AND GENTLE

But we were gentle among you, just as a

nursing mother cherishes her own children.
(1 Thessalonians 2:6–7)

It's interesting to note that out of all the words Paul might have used to show affection, he chose one we can all understand. *Mother.* When the apostle speaks of how a mom cherishes her children, he uses a term that speaks of "affectionate longing." It's when you feel yourself drawn to something or someone.

When applied to a dad, it's a father who holds and treats the little child tenderly, feeling drawn to that little one. I remember when I first held both of my sons. They were so tiny, so sweet, so vulnerable. It was hard to imagine either of them as adults. Now my oldest is almost as tall as I am. But I can still vividly remember him as an infant and a child.

These children grow so quickly!

Billy Graham was recently asked, "What has been the biggest surprise of your life?"

"The brevity of it," he replied.

By the way, this closeness, this tenderness, this fond affection for our children *isn't supposed to end as they grow up.* Yes, they need it and crave it when they are tiny and vulnerable. But guess what? They need it just as much when they are bigger than you are! We need to continue to love and care for them through their different stages of development.

Paul went on to say, "We loved you so much that we gave you not only God's Good News but our own lives, too" (v. 8, NLT).

There is no greater joy than to see our children embrace Christ as their own Savior. In that moment it becomes a personal faith, not just the faith of Dad and Mom.

Shortly before his death, David said to his son Solomon,

> "As for you, my son Solomon, know the God of your father, and serve Him with a loyal heart and with a willing mind; for the Lord searches all hearts and understands all the intent of the thoughts. If you seek Him, He will be found by you; but if you forsake Him, He will cast you off forever."
> (1 Chronicles 28:9)

As the apostle John said, "I have no greater joy than to hear that my children walk in truth" (3 John 1:4).

HOW DO WE REACH OUR CHILDREN FOR CHRIST?

Our children need to see the Gospel lived as well as preached. In fact, when we live "two lives," we contradict what we say we teach our children as well. We teach them the wrong thing!

Know this, dads. You *are* an example.

That fact was established and settled when you conceived a child. It doesn't matter if you don't want to be one. You can't escape it. In fact, you're an example even in your *absence*. The question is, what kind of example do you want to be? It's a sad and serious thing to never speak to your children about a relationship with God, but it's an even worse thing to tell them and then blatantly contradict those words in self-centered, hypocritical living.

So…in leading the way and setting the example, we begin to model an authentically Christian lifestyle. It's not a matter of being "perfect." It's a matter of turning to the Lord and depending on Him in any and every circumstance of life.

So your children see you overwhelmed and under pressure? *Show them how a man of God admits his need, and depends on the Lord for strength far beyond his own.*

So your children see you stumble? *Show them how to get a fresh grip on God's grace and stand up again.*

So your children see you fail? *Show them how to admit to that failure, seek God's forgiveness and restoration, and climb back into the saddle.*

So your children see you go through spiritual dry times? *Show them how to live a life of faith, regardless of setbacks.*

Believe it or not, many years from now, having your son or daughter say, "Dad did everything right," won't be nearly as helpful as having them recall, "You know, Dad didn't get everything right, and he really messed up sometimes. But I'll never forget how he turned to the Lord for everything, and depended on God every day."

Andrew Murray wrote: "The secret of home rule is self-rule, first being ourselves what we want our children to be."

SEIZING EVERY OPPORTUNITY

When Moses spoke to the Israelites shortly before his death, he declared, "Hear, O Israel...You shall love the Lord your God with all your heart, with all your soul, and with all your strength. And these words which I command you today shall be in your heart. You shall teach them diligently to your children, and shall talk of them when you sit in your house, when you walk by the way, when you lie down, and when you rise up." (Deuteronomy 6:4–7)

First, we must develop our own fellowship and relationship with God. We cannot lead a child any further than we have come. We then teach the Word naturally and spontaneously to our children, the way Jesus taught.

When the Lord taught His men lessons about life, it wasn't in a classroom. He wasn't standing at a lectern with the Twelve sitting on folding chairs in a semi-circle. It was out on the road…walking through the fields…strolling through the temple… reclining on a sunny hillside overlooking the sea… sitting by a crackling campfire at night.

When He began teaching the crucial lesson of how to share in His very life, He didn't use any overheads or PowerPoint® presentations. He simply drew truths from the common, everyday things all around them in their environment.

When He said, "I am the true vine, and My

Father is the vinedresser…" He wasn't lecturing in a classroom, looking for an appropriate metaphor. *They were very likely walking through an actual vineyard.*

When Jesus spoke to the Samaritan woman about finding living water that would satisfy her deepest thirst, they weren't in a counseling office with New Age music and indirect lighting, *they were standing by a well in the heat of the day.*

When Jesus told Nicodemus about the mystery of God's Spirit, comparing Him to wind, they weren't communicating in some kind of on-line training session over the Internet. *They were standing on a rooftop at night, with a soft evening breeze whispering through the palm leaves and ruffling their hair.*

Every day, every hour you spend with your kids is an opportunity for informal teaching. But if the only time you ever see them is right before they rush off for school in the morning or right before they hit the sack at night, it's going to be difficult to teach those spontaneous life lessons as Jesus did.

How about a walk after dinner?

How about a Saturday morning stroll along the beach or a lakeside?

How about a summer hike or backpack in the woods?

How about taking one of the kids with you in the car when you run your errands?

It simply means giving it some extra thought, and doing whatever it takes to help your boys and girls, your young men and women, begin to integrate God's truth into their natural lifestyle. Once again, it is teaching that is spontaneous (not structured and planned), natural (not forced or "religious"), and constant (not hit or miss when you happen to think about it).

Men, I am calling on you today to be the fathers God has called you to be. You can't even think about deserting. You are on the front lines. Your children need you. Your country needs you. The church of Jesus Christ needs you…and the time you invest will shape lives for all of eternity.

The Mother Who
Wouldn't Give Up

Have you every prayed with all of your heart for something you believed to be the will of God, and heard…nothing? Nothing but an apparent "icy silence" from heaven?

Perhaps it was for the salvation of a loved one.

Maybe it was for God's provision when times were tight.

Many of us have prayed to pass a big exam in school.

It may be that you've been praying for a life companion, but there's no one on the horizon.

Possibly you were crying out for His healing touch in your life at a time when your health was in danger.

If you have prayed in such a way, you will find much in common with the woman in the story before us. She was a mother who would not give up. It is a story that not only gives hope to mothers who care for the well being of their children, it also stands as an encouragement to all of us that the very things we consider barriers in our path may actually be bridges to blessings of God beyond our imagination.

> Then Jesus went out from there and departed to the region of Tyre and Sidon. And behold, a woman of Canaan came from that region and cried out to Him, saying, "Have mercy on me, O Lord, Son of David! My daughter is severely demon-possessed."

> But He answered her not a word.

> And His disciples came and urged Him, saying, "Send her away, for she cries out after us."

> But He answered and said, "I was not sent except to the lost sheep of the house of Israel."

> Then she came and worshiped Him, saying, "Lord, help me!"

> But He answered and said, "It is not good to take the children's bread and throw it to the little dogs."

And she said, "Yes, Lord, yet even the little dogs eat the crumbs which fall from their masters' table."

Then Jesus answered and said to her, "O woman, great is your faith! Let it be to you as you desire." And her daughter was healed from that very hour. (Matthew 15:21–28)

DID JESUS INSULT A WOMAN?

Without an understanding of the language and culture of that day, it could appear that Jesus was initially "blowing this woman off," and rejecting her. But keep in mind that Jesus responded to this woman in such a way, not because He wanted to destroy her faith, but rather to develop it. He was not playing games with this Gentile lady, nor was He trying to make a difficult situation even more difficult for her.

In fact, He was drawing out her faith. He knew she would "rise to the challenge," and stand as an example of belief and persistence in prayer for His own disciples—including you and me—to learn from.

Let's first consider who this woman was.

The Bible calls her "a woman of Canaan." This means she was a non-Jew, a Gentile. Mark tells us she was a Greek, born in Syrian Phoenicia. Living when and where she lived, she very well could have been a worshiper of "Astarte," the goddess of fertility, and other pagan deities in that region.

Why, then, did she come to Jesus? Why did she so persistently seek out the Lord and pray to Him? Could she have been disillusioned with the pagan "gods," who always seemed to take but never give? Somehow, she'd gotten word of a young Jew, a descendant of King David, who performed signs and wonders, and stood up to the religious authorities of Israel. Could this be the Messiah, the Christ spoken of in Scripture?

This woman, never named in Scripture, had a daughter who had come under the power of demon spirits. In her mother's words, her girl was "severely demon-possessed." How she ended up this way, we don't know. We might assume it was because of the mother's pagan involvement up to that point with demonic influence that had an adverse affect on her daughter. Perhaps there had been many little idols and gods in the home as the little girl grew up, and this had opened up a doorway to devilish power in her life.

It's a reminder to us that we do have a direct influence on our children. The scriptural truth still holds today that says the sins of the parents are visited upon the children (Exodus 20:5). We see it in our society as particular crimes and sins are passed from generation to generation. It's certainly true with alcoholism. Children of alcoholics are four to six times more likely than the general population to develop alcohol problems. Growing up, these children see that when the pressure is on, Mom and Dad turn to the bottle...and now they do the same.

In addition, anxiety and depression are more common among children of alcoholics (COAs) than among children of non-alcoholics. It's the same for boys and girls who are raised in physically and verbally abusive homes; when the children grow up and have children of their own, they tend to follow that same destructive pattern. It's also been clearly established that children coming from homes where the parents divorced have far higher rates of depression, poor performance in school, and out of wedlock births, carrying their intense inner pain and bitterness well into their adult years. Ironically, even after all they have suffered, they are far more likely to divorce than children from intact homes.

As a pastor who has dealt with many, many sad situations, I have to say that it's not uncommon for *all* of these problems to be present: alcoholism, abuse, and divorce.

We don't live to ourselves alone. The choices we make are not choices that affect us alone, as much as we may want to believe that. We as parents need to think very carefully and soberly about our impact on the lives of our children! (In all fairness, there are also kids who are raised in wonderful, godly homes that get themselves into all kinds of trouble as well. Even though that may be true, you have still laid a godly foundation for their lives, to which they may one day return.)

JESUS TAKES A "SIDE TRIP"

Whatever the case with this Greek woman, one thing was for sure. Her daughter was in trouble and only Jesus could help her. It's also worth noting that Jesus' visit to Tyre and Sidon on the coast is the only occasion where He left His own country. The crowds back home were huge. The speculation and excitement level about His person and ministry had reached a fever pitch. His disciples were ready to establish the kingdom at any moment.

And Jesus picked that moment to leave the country.

Why go all the way to the coast of the Great Sea, when His ministry had been solely devoted to Jewish people in Israel? Why travel so far at that particular moment in His brief ministry?

Scripture lists only one reason for His doing so.

It would appear He had an appointment with a poor, desperate woman who was hungry for an encounter with the true and living God. As with the "woman at the well," Jesus seemed to go out of His way that she might find Him. When she did come before Jesus, she had an accurate assessment of her own spiritual condition: She didn't demand a thing, but only cried out to Him for mercy.

This woman, like any loving mother, loved her child more than her own life. And finding Jesus, she pleaded,

> "Have mercy on me, O Lord, Son of David!
> My daughter is severely demon-possessed."

> But He answered her not a word. (vv. 22–23)

Again, without an understanding of the culture

of this day and the original language, it seems as though Jesus was being rather flippant with her, even disinterested. The disciples apparently interpreted Jesus' ignoring the woman as a sign of unconcern, and wondered why He didn't just send her away.

The word Matthew uses for "cried out" in this account doesn't imply a polite, timid, little whimper. The term comes from a verb that literally means to "croak" or scream as a raven. Shades of meaning include words like *shriek*, *exclaim*, and *entreat*.

It was obviously grating on the disciples' nerves. As the minutes passed, and the woman continued shrieking and following them about, the Lord's men became more and more upset and irritated. It must have been creating something of a scene, perhaps embarrassing them. You can just see them looking back over their shoulders, rolling their eyes at each other, and whispering among themselves, "Why doesn't He just get rid of her?"

Jesus, however, didn't even seem to notice. The woman's screams might as well have been the chirping of a songbird or the whistling of the wind. He didn't acknowledge her presence, and seemed completely preoccupied or disinterested.

But nothing could be further from the truth.

Jesus could sense the great faith that overflowed from her heart. He was well aware of every nuance of that situation—including His disciples' irritation and jangled nerves.

Sometimes the hardest response to accept is no response at all, and that's what this woman received from Jesus. *"He did not answer her a word."* But that didn't mean He wasn't listening— nor did it mean He wouldn't answer her prayer. He'd had enough superficiality and phoniness back in Judea; over here on the Gentile coastline, He wanted to test this woman's faith, showcasing her as an example to His sometimes-doubting disciples.

THE PURPOSE OF HIS BARRIERS

He didn't put up those barriers of silence and apparent indifference to keep this woman away, but to actually draw her closer! He erected barriers that only genuine, persistent faith could hurdle—a heart that refused to give up.

There are similarities between this encounter and the Lord's conversation with the rich young ruler—but with tragically different results. Jesus also set up barriers for this young man, but in his case, the barriers turned him away. Why? Because he didn't have nearly as much desire or persistence as the Gentile woman. For all his outward, breathless eagerness, his faith was superficial and his expressed desire for eternal life didn't go deep enough.

> Now a certain ruler asked Him, saying, "Good Teacher, what shall I do to inherit eternal life?"

> So Jesus said to him, "Why do you call Me good? No one is good but One, that is, God. You know the commandments: 'Do not commit adultery,' 'Do not murder,' 'Do not steal,' 'Do not bear false witness,' 'Honor your father and your mother.'"

> And he said, "All these things I have kept from my youth."

> So when Jesus heard these things, He said to him, "You still lack one thing. Sell all that you have and distribute to the poor, and you will have treasure in heaven; and come, follow Me."

But when he heard this, he became very
sorrowful, for he was very rich.
(Luke 18:18–23)

This wasn't about money, as much as it was
about this young man's *heart*. There was nothing
wrong with the fact that he had possessions. The
problem lay in the fact that his possessions seemed
to possess him!

The Bible warns us that "covetousness is
idolatry." And in this young man's life, that
certainly seems to be the case. Jesus was trying to
draw him out, to bring him to a point of decision,
to clearly lay out the spiritual issues before him.
Again, He erected barriers that only genuine,
persistent faith could hurdle. But sadly, this
wealthy young man of the ruling class did not "rise
to the challenge."

Coming back to the woman from Syrian
Phoenicia, look at what the Lord said to her in
response to her plea, "Lord, help me!"

"It is not good to take the children's bread
and throw it to the dogs." (v. 26)

Dogs? What kind of response was that? As it
happens, there are two different Greek words for
dogs. The first word refers to the mangy, dirty

packs of dogs that roamed about in that part of the world, living off of garbage and dead animals. That's not the kind of dog Jesus refers to here. The second word refers to little puppies or family pets—and that's the term Jesus used.

Puppies are so cute. Well, I guess kittens are, too. But puppies grow up to be dogs, and kittens become cats. Sometimes people get carried away with little cute animals. At Easter some folks are charmed by the cute yellow chicks and little bunnies, but before they know it their house is overrun with rabbits and chickens. At that moment, rabbit stew and Chicken McNuggets® are starting to sound real good!

Even though Jesus used the more affectionate term for dog here, it was still hardly a compliment! A dog is still a dog. But this lady wasn't deterred at all. I'm sure she totally understood what was going on here. She knew very well Jesus had what she needed. She knew He could heal her beloved daughter with a single word. She could also see the love in the Galilean's eyes behind the apparent indifference. She could hear the compassion in His voice.

So she came back with the classic response in

verse 27: "Yes, Lord, yet even the little dogs eat the crumbs which fall from their masters' table."

Bingo! This is exactly what the Lord was waiting for.

Her faith was so great she realized *even a tiny leftover of Jesus' power would be enough to heal her daughter.* I believe a smile came over His face, as she rose to His challenge. After putting up a barrier of silence and then a double barrier of seeming rejection, Jesus heard what He wanted to hear.

Remember, this is the same God who said, "Then you will call upon Me and go and pray to Me, and I will listen to you. And you will seek Me and find Me, when you search for Me with all your heart. I will be found by you, says the LORD" (Jeremiah 29:12–14).

In an instant, Jesus dramatically changed the way He had been dealing with this woman, turning from apparent rejection of her to giving her a virtual "carte blanche."

Why? For a number of reasons.

You mothers who have been praying for something you believe to be the will of God should note this. You've been seeking God's face concerning the salvation of your husband or your children, or you've been praying that God will get hold of their hearts and set them on fire to serve Him. Look at the Lord's amazing statement to this Gentile woman in verse 28:

> "O woman, great is your faith! Let it be to you as you desire."

I think the disciples' mouths must have dropped open at this point. *Let it be to you as you desire?* What was going on here? Why this sudden turnaround? Why was He even speaking to a Gentile woman? One moment He was ignoring her (which made perfect sense to them), and the next moment He was offering her *whatever she wanted*.

THE BLANK CHECK

What would you say if the Lord suddenly made an offer like that to you?

I heard the story of a beachcomber strolling along a California beach one day and noticing the end of a bottle protruding from the sand. Pulling it out, he was surprised to see that it was made of something heavy—some kind of metal or stone. And it was encrusted with jewels! Excitedly knocking the gritty sand off its surface to get a better look, he was stunned when multi-colored smoke began pouring from the bottle and a genie appeared. As is customary in such situations, the genie offered the man three wishes.

The beachcomber thought about it for awhile. Finally he said, "You know, I have always wanted to go to Hawaii, but I'm afraid to fly, and afraid to go on a ship. So my first wish is for a highway from here to Hawaii." Now it was the genie's turn to be surprised. What kind of request was that? Didn't the man want gold? Money? Fame? Glory? Property? No, the man insisted, he wanted a highway to Hawaii.

The genie patiently explained that this was virtually impossible. The time, resources, and energy required for such a thing would leave the genie drained for thousands of years. "Isn't there something else you might want?" he asked.

The man paused again to think. Finally, he said, "Well, I have always wanted to understand women…."

And the genie replied, "So…on this highway. Did you want two lanes or four?"

We've all heard variations on the "three wishes"

story, whether it's a genie or a fairy godmother. There was a time in the life of King Solomon however, early in his reign, when the Lord came to him at night and offered him whatever he wanted.

> At Gibeon the Lord appeared to Solomon in a dream by night; and God said, "Ask! What shall I give you?" (1 Kings 3:5)

It was a blank check.

Now if I handed you a blank check, it wouldn't be that big of a deal. You'd be limited to whatever I happened to have in my checking account—which might not be worth your while. But if *God* hands you a blank check, you'll be drawing from the Bank of Heaven—and no one has ever tapped out *that* account.

But the truth is, God would never offer something like this to a person who wasn't ready for it. You don't give a high-performance sports car to an eight-year-old. He isn't ready for it. Even if he could reach the pedals or see over the steering wheel, it wouldn't be good for him! And God wouldn't say, *"Ask! What shall I give you?"* to someone whose heart wasn't in the right place. But because Solomon had his priorities in order as a young man who loved the Lord, he asked for what

God really wanted him to have—*wisdom* to lead God's people.

Perhaps you wish the Lord would come to you and offer such a thing. I'm not so sure I would want it. I've always found it best to let God choose for me. And why is that? Because He is infinitely wiser than I am. And besides that, I know His heart. In Jeremiah 29:11 (NIV), He tells the exiles in Babylon: "For I know the plans I have for you...plans to prosper you and not to harm you, plans to give you hope and a future."

Why wouldn't I leave a decision like that to a God who loves me with an infinite love? Why wouldn't I trust a God who gave up His own Son for me to make me His child and give me eternal life in heaven?

The apostle Paul asked a very similar question: "What then shall we say to these things? If God is for us, who can be against us? He who did not spare His own Son, but delivered Him up for us all, how shall He not with Him also freely give us all things?" (Romans 8:31–32).

If He would do that for me, if He would allow His Son to be shamed, tortured, brutalized, and die a terrible death to pay a debt I could never pay, why wouldn't I trust such a God to provide whatever else I needed in life?

"I WON'T LET YOU GO"

So why was this great privilege of "asking for anything" given to this common woman who wasn't even one of the chosen people?

It was because of her persistence, tenacity, commitment…and most of all, her faith. When the door was shut in her face, she stood there knocking on it. When Jesus called her "dog," she only picked up what He had said, like a good dog would pick up his master's stick and bring it right to his feet. She had such faith that she simply would not go home without it.

Apart from Jesus, there was no hope for her tormented girl. And in that moment, she may have been like Simon Peter who once said to Jesus, "Lord, to whom would we go? You alone have the words that give eternal life. We believe them, and we know you are the Holy One of God" (John 6:68, NLT).

When I read this story, I'm reminded of the Old Testament account of Jacob, rascal and conniver that he was, who wrestled all night with God and said, "I won't let You go till You bless me." That's the heart attitude of this lady from Canaan. If she didn't get her answer the first time around, she would keep asking, seeking, and knocking until she did. *"Lord, I won't stop following You and calling out for mercy till You bless me!"* I can picture her following Jesus all the way back to Galilee.

She loved her child more than life itself…and she had no idea if or when Jesus might be by this way again.

In fact, as far as we know, He never did go back. He'd never been there before, and His path would never lead that way again. And while the Messiah was in the neighborhood, this woman was not going to miss her chance.

Now, we know that God is always with us. One of His most amazing attributes is His "omnipresence." He is present everywhere at once, and there is no place where He is not. But there are times in life when we are more aware of Him than at other times. These are times when we see Him more clearly with the eyes of faith, times when we sense His presence and nearness in an unusual way. In those moments, He seems closer to us. Ready to listen. Ready to hear. Ready to minister to our needs.

Don't waste moments like that! Pursue Him in such times with all your heart. Keep crying out to Him and follow Him as closely as You can. The Bible says, "Seek the LORD while He may be found, call upon Him while He is near" (Isaiah 55:6).

Do you ever feel the Holy Spirit prompting your heart to draw near to God, to spend time with Him? Do you ever hear that "still, small voice" inviting You to seek God's face in prayer? Respond to that summons! Don't put it off. Ten minutes from now, you may lose that sense of urgency, that awareness of His presence, and get preoccupied with something else.

This Gentile woman took full advantage of her opportunity to be with Jesus. She took advantage of His nearness and cried out to Him for her troubled daughter.

In that sense, she was acting as a true intercessor! One time when Moses was praying for God to spare Israel, in spite of their rebellion, he cried out to God, "Oh, these people have committed a great sin, and have made for themselves a god of gold! Yet now, if You will forgive their sin—but if not, I pray, blot me out of Your book which You have written" (Exodus 32:31–32).

What an example for us as parents to not give up when praying for our children. Maybe your son or daughter has taken a prodigal turn. The sad truth is they may have to hit bottom before they see their need for God. Don't give up, and don't feel like God has abandoned you or failed you. Keep praying. Be like this woman and *stay with it*! Your children can escape your presence, but they cannot escape your prayers.

J. Sidlow Baxter once wrote, "Men may spurn our appeals, reject our message, oppose our arguments, despise our persons—but they are helpless against our prayers!" Don't let the devil whisper in your ear, "It's too late for them. *They will never change.*" That's the father of lies speaking to you in those moments. The truth is, it's *not* too late. After all, you want them to be saved, and God wants to save them. Jesus gave up His life on the cross to save them. So keep at it until you see the change in their lives.

COMING INTO ALIGNMENT

The second reason Jesus gave this woman everything she asked for was because she got her will in alignment with His.

There are many times that as a mother—or father or grandparent—*you just don't know how to pray.*

If you had been Rachel, Joseph's mother, you no doubt would have prayed that God would keep him safe. How could you know that the hard times in this young man's future would work together for a great, great good? You would not have prayed, "Lord, I pray that my son Joseph is hated by his brothers, and then sold into slavery, and falsely accused of raping a woman, and then thrown into prison." What mother in her right mind would pray a prayer like that? But God allowed those circumstances in Joseph's life to bring about His will.

Had you been Daniel's mother, surely you would have prayed that Israel would never be taken captive. How could she know that her little "Danny boy," kidnapped by the Babylonians, would one day become one of Israel's mightiest prophets, and stand in the court of great and powerful kings?

Had you been Mary, how easily you could have prayed, "Oh dear Father, no! Not crucifixion! Anything but that!" Imagine if you will how hard that must have been for Mary to see her

Son hanging on a bloody cross, beaten beyond recognition. She had guided those once tiny hands, and counted the toes on those once tiny feet, that now had spikes driven through them. She had lovingly caressed that head that was covered with a crude crown of thorns. Oh, the pain and the anguish! It was as Simeon had prophesied to Mary when Jesus was just an infant: "Yes, a sword will pierce through your own soul, also" (Luke 2:35).

And even as He was dying on that cross, Jesus looked down at His mother with great tenderness, asking the apostle John to care for her. It was cruelly hard to bear. But it was through His death that the world would be saved—including Mary herself. No, God in His infinite love and wisdom does not answer all the prayers even of a loving mother, because He may have something different and better in mind. So, go ahead and pray for the blessing and protection of God on your children. But always add a little "P.S." to your prayers: "Your kingdom come, Your will be done…." Why? Because those barriers you see in the lives of your children today may become "bridges to blessings" tomorrow.

The key is to get our will in alignment with

His! For true praying is not overcoming God's reluctance but laying hold of His willingness! Martin Luther once said: "By our praying, we are instructing ourselves more than Him." The Bible says, "Whatever we ask we receive from Him, because we keep His commandments and do those things that are pleasing in His sight" (1 John 3:22).

If we give a listening ear to all God's commands to us, He will give a listening ear to all our prayers to Him.

Know this! Jesus won't offer this "carte blanche" to just anyone. Those who think only of themselves or are motivated by greed need not apply! It is to the humble person, who is not questioning God's will but rather surrendering to it, He offers such a possibility.

When He called this woman a dog, she did not take offense. She said, "Yes, Lord, but even the little dogs…." If you will agree with Him He will agree with you. If you do not yield to Him He will not yield to you. Spurgeon said, "When you have great desires for heavenly things, when your desires are such as God approves of, when you will what God wills, then you will have what you like."

Now let's consider this blank check from God.

What do you really want? The salvation of your child, your husband, wife, your friend, even your enemy? You're right on track! God wants that, too. So don't give up, persist! Remember, what may appear to be indifference on the part of God is nothing of the sort, but rather a barrier He wishes you to overcome by persistent faith! He does not put up these barriers to *keep us away, but to draw us closer.* He erects barriers that only genuine, persistent faith can hurdle.

So let's learn a lesson today from the "mother who wouldn't give up"!

Jesus said, "Men always ought to pray and not lose heart" (Luke 18:1).

It's always too early to give up, and never too late to touch His heart of mercy.

9

How to Divorce-Proof
Your Marriage

A number of years ago there was a television program called, "Who Wants to Marry a Millionaire?" Never mind if you didn't get to see it. You really didn't miss much.

As the show began, fifty women were chosen from a pool of over three thousand to have the privilege of not just meeting, but marrying (sight unseen), a genuine, living, breathing millionaire.

As part of the competition there was a "beachwear contest," because, host Jay Thomas rationalized, Mr. Moneybags wanted his lady-love to be "as comfortable on the beach as he is." There was also a "personality test," in which ten semi-finalists answered intelligent, perceptive questions such as: *How would you spend his money?* And, *Would you mind if he went to "strip clubs"?*

As the women were interviewed, millionaire Rick Rockwell watched from a high-tech perch.

The ultimate winner was a nurse named Darva Conger who, along with the new husband she had just met, walked away with more than $100,000 in loot, including a new SUV and a $35,000 three-carat diamond ring.

What's next for so-called "reality TV"? *Who Wants to Sell Your Soul?* The newlyweds quickly headed for divorce court—or at least an annulment. Interviewed on "Good Morning America," blushing bride Darva said, "I don't think I was thinking clearly, I committed an error in judgment." (Right. Just a "small misjudgment" like double parking…or maybe forgetting to click into a seatbelt.) She said she didn't want to disparage her husband, Mr. Rockwell, but after spending some time with him she concluded, "I was very uncomfortable around him. He's just not a person that I would ordinarily have a friendly relationship with."

She said they spent their "honeymoon" in separate rooms, and she told him, "I am not married to you. In my heart, I'm not married to you." To everyone who thought the show debased the institution of marriage, Rockwell said he "really had a romantic ideal" in his mind, but he agreed an annulment was likely. It turns out that "Prince Charming" had a restraining order against him—for hitting an old girlfriend and threatening her life.

What happened to this storybook marriage? You're telling me a TV reality show isn't the perfect foundation for a long-lasting relationship? What a shock!

Now we can laugh at something as ridiculous and far-fetched as this. Yet tragically, marriages that have lasted for five, ten, even twenty years are falling apart at a record rate. This breakdown of the family has sent shock waves across our whole nation.

When we tamper with God's plan, we do so at our own peril.

BREAKING THE CYCLE

Not only is divorce devastating to the husband and wife, but it is unbelievably damaging and destructive in the lives of children. "Kids are resilient," we hear people say. "They'll bounce back."

But it's a lie.

Nobody ever completely bounces back from the

rending of a family.

Dr. Armand Nicholi, a respected professor at the Harvard Medical School and a staff physician at Massachusetts General Hospital, said, "The breakdown of the family contributes significantly to the major problems confronting our society today. Research data make unmistakably clear a strong relationship between broken families and the drug epidemic, the increase of violent crime, and the unprecedented epidemic of suicide among children and adolescents."

In a very real way, as the Scripture says, "the sins of the parents are visited upon the children." According to *Father Facts*, a publication of the National Fatherhood Initiative, children of divorce are much more likely to drop out of school, to engage in premarital sex, and to become pregnant than children of intact families.

Consider this one telling fact: Seventy percent of children in state reform institutions grew up in single-parent homes. An article from *Newsweek* magazine from a number of years ago, entitled, "Breaking the Divorce Cycle," details how the children of broken marriages carry deep wounds well into their adult lives.

The article goes on to say: "Divorce remains a central issue throughout their lives, no matter how well adjusted they may seem to be. A hole in the heart is universal; there is a sense of having missed out on something that is a birthright, the right to grow up in a house with two parents. Compared with people who have grown up in intact families, adult children of divorce are more likely to have troubled relationships and broken marriages. A desire for stability sends some down the aisle at too young an age, and they end up in divorce court not long afterward."

So you see, the cycle can continue from generation to generation.

Yet in spite of these alarming statistics, the divorce rate rose *seven hundred percent* in the twentieth century, and hasn't begun to top out in Century 21. There is now one divorce for every 1.8 marriages. Over a million children a year are involved in divorce cases. In Tampa, Florida you can now get a divorce without leaving your car— drive thru divorces.

DIVORCE IN THE FAMILY OF GOD

I wish I could say this was only true of

nonbelievers. But that's just not the case. The hard truth is that divorce is escalating in the church today. George Barna recently conducted a survey on divorce in the church. According to this nationwide survey of nearly 4,000 adults, 27 percent of born-again Christians are currently or have previously been divorced, compared to 24 percent among adults who are not born-again. When it was suggested that perhaps the reason these numbers skewed so high was because the Christians who were polled were divorced before their conversions, Barna pointed out that 9 out of 10 Christians who had been divorced went through the divorce process *after* they had accepted Christ. That means that 1 out of every 4 Christians has been divorced.

I'm not saying that divorce could never happen in a Christian marriage. There are indeed scriptural grounds for it, including unfaithfulness. But unfaithfulness is not only grounds for divorce, it's also grounds for forgiveness! As a follower of Jesus Christ you should avoid divorce with everything within you. For you have no idea of the potential devastation it can cause, not only now, but for many years to come.

I once heard John MacArthur say, "Some think divorce is a confusing subject. If there is confusion about the subject of divorce and remarriage, it's not because God has given us a confused word in Scripture. The confusion arises when we try to accommodate the divine standard to the lack of standards in our contemporary morality."

And that is so true.

The Big Question is this: Are we going to live according to the teachings of God's Word, or are we going to let this world squeeze us into its mold? Now I realize that if you are a Christian who has been divorced or is in the process of getting a divorce, you're sorely tempted about now to toss this book aside—or at least skip to the next chapter. You're thinking that I, the author, am going to make your life miserable for the next few pages.

But that's not necessarily the case.

Because divorce is not always wrong.

God has clearly given us "release clauses" that I want to identify. At the same time, I do think most marriages that have had so-called "irreconcilable differences" could have been saved. Yes, if it's done, it's done—unless there is a chance at reconciliation. But I am primarily addressing my comments to those who are married and are thinking about marriage. I want to do everything I can to encourage you to stay in that relationship.

PROTECTION FROM THE FLAMES

I've called this chapter, "How to Divorce-Proof Your Marriage." But the fact of the matter is, no couple can have a one hundred percent guarantee that their marriage will never fall apart. Having said that, it is also true that there are some very practical, "no-brainer" steps you can take to protect your home from the plague of divorce that has swept across our country.

After one of the devastating wildfires that roar through Southern California from time to time, I saw a dramatic photo in the newspaper of an entire neighborhood with nothing remaining but the foundations of twenty homes. In the midst of all this, however, with burned-out homes to the left and right, one house stood alone. It was darkened a bit by all the smoke, but it escaped unscathed.

The man who had built the house was interviewed as to why this happened. "We went beyond what was required," he said, "and made it even safer: That included double-paned windows, thick stucco walls, sealed eves, concrete tile roof and abundant insulation." Firefighters chose that spot, in front of this man's home, to make a stand.

Now you or I can't personally stop the wildfire of divorce in our culture today, but we can take practical steps to "fireproof" our own house! As that man said, "We went beyond what was required to make it even safer."

And please hear me on this: divorce can be more destructive and devastating than a raging wildfire. Those burned-out homes I saw in the paper have been rebuilt. If you would walk down that street today, you would look in vain for the damage and devastation. But the power of a divorce to tear lives and shred souls and pierce the hearts of children may not be healed for generations— perhaps not in a hundred years, if that.

You might say, "Greg, there's no way to stop this divorce escalation in our culture. It's like a runaway freight train. How are you going to put the brakes to a societal trend as big as that?"

I might simply answer that question with another question. *How do you eat an elephant?* Now that's something I've never attempted, but if I ever had it to do, I'd pick up my fork in one hand, a bottle of ketchup in the other, and eat the thing *one bite at a time.*

The first thing we must do is make sure divorce never happens under *our* roof. Like the firefighters in front of the fire protected home, we must take our stand at our own driveway, and say to those flames—even if they are the flames of hell—*"Not now! Not here! Not at THIS house!"*

While addressing this crucial subject of marriage with the believers in Ephesus, Paul wrote: "For this reason a man shall leave his father and mother and be joined to his wife, and the two shall become one flesh" (Ephesians 5:31). Now what Paul was really doing here was reciting a memory verse—from the second chapter of Genesis.

God had placed Adam in the Garden with about as sweet a job description as one could have. There used to be a comic strip called, "L'il Abner." And in that strip, the hero's job was a mattress tester at the local mattress factory. But Adam's job was even better than that! His occupation was to tend and discover the secrets of that incredible garden, and to enjoy fellowship with God Himself, who apparently came walking in that garden every twilight.

But in spite of all this there was something missing in Adam's life.

A companion with whom to share all this beauty and joy.

HELP IS ON THE WAY

Over and over, as God created marvel after marvel, we read that He "saw that it was good…" But when the Lord looked at Adam's loneliness, He said, "It is not good that man should be alone; I will make him a helper comparable to him" (Genesis 2:18).

The term "helper" in the original language speaks of "someone who assists another to reach fulfillment." It is used elsewhere in the Old Testament when referring to someone coming to "rescue another."

This phrase "comparable to him" could also be translated "suitable to him." Literally, "corresponding to him." She would provide what was missing in his life.

Let's take another look at that foundational document of Genesis for just a little more detail:

So Adam gave names to all cattle, to the birds of the air, and to every beast of the field. But for Adam there was not found a helper comparable to him.

And the Lord God caused a deep sleep to fall on Adam, and he slept; and He took one of his ribs, and closed up the flesh in its place. Then the rib which the Lord God had taken from man He made into a woman, and He brought her to the man.

And Adam said:

"This is now bone of my bones
And flesh of my flesh;
She shall be called Woman,
Because she was taken out of Man."

Therefore a man shall leave his father and mother and be joined to his wife, and they shall become one flesh.
(Genesis 2:21–24)

So God made Eve from the rib of Adam.

One thing you may not know is that Eve was suspicious of Adam. When Adam stayed out very late for a few nights, Eve became upset. "You're running around with other women," she charged.

Adam responded, "Eve, are you crazy? You're

the only woman on earth."

This argument continued until Adam fell asleep, only to be awakened be someone poking him in the side. It was Eve.

"What do you think you're doing?" Adam demanded.

"Counting your ribs," Eve said.

Matthew Henry writes: "Eve was made by God not out of his head to rule over him, nor out of his feet to be trampled upon by him, but out of his side to be equal with him, under his arm to be protected, and near his heart to be loved."

LEAVE AND CLEAVE

The words "leaving" and "cleaving" are opposites, tied together as the process of establishing a new union, a new home, a new family.

Leave and cleave.

Sever and bond.

Loosen and secure.

Depart from and attach to.

The Hebrew term translated "cleave" means "to glue, to cling." Have you ever used any of that mega-bonding, permanent-welding super glue? It's handy stuff to have around, but when you're trying to hold two broken pieces of something together, I still haven't figured out how to keep from bonding my index finger to my thumb. To get yourself free, you almost have to transfer your thumbprint to your finger—or maybe the other way around.

But before that cleaving in a marriage can take place, there has to be a leaving—leaving all other relationships. The closest relationship outside of marriage is specified here, implying that if it is necessary to leave your father and mother, then certainly all lesser ties must be broken, changed, or left behind. The man's primary commitment must be to his wife (and hers to him). He must continue to honor his parents, but the relationship can never be the same. There has to be a distinct separation. Otherwise this can be extremely detrimental to the marriage.

Some men and women find it very hard to break free like this. I heard the story of one single young man who wanted to get married in the worst way. He brought home a young lady but his mother didn't like her. He proceeded to bring home a second girl, but his mother didn't like her, either. This happened two more times. Finally he found a girl who looked like his mother, dressed like her, talked like her, and acted like her. But when he brought her home to meet his parents, his *father* didn't like her!

This process of "leaving" also means a distinct change in relationships of a lesser degree of importance. Frankly, best friends can become a real problem. No matter how close that relationship may have been, it has to change! There has to be that acknowledgment that "life is different now." Your spouse is not only to be your companion and lover, but also your friend. And your "best friend" at that!

There is a key verse in Scripture that emphasizes the importance of friendship between spouses. In Malachi 2:13, the prophet says, "The LORD has been witness between you and the wife of your youth in whom you have been faithless, although she is your companion and wife."

What is a companion? It is "one with whom you are united in thoughts, goals, plans, and efforts." Many men don't really have a close friendship with their wives. This is not only unfortunate and sad, it is unscriptural. It is a direct contradiction of God's good and wise plan.

"Leaving" also means giving other

preoccupations in life a lesser priority. Your business, career, house, hobbies, interests—even church work. Your new order of priority in life is 1) God; 2) family; and 3) service.

It's no use leaving unless you are willing to spend a lifetime cleaving. "Becoming one flesh" suggests a process, a lifelong pursuit, not merely an instant fact.

To cleave means to "adhere to, stick to, or be attached by some strong tie." The verb suggests "a determined action." So there is nothing sloppy, lazy, or passive about the act of cleaving. Think of it more in terms of climbing a mountain. It always takes effort, you keep moving up, and the view gets better and better the higher you go.

When we come to the New Testament use of the word, the Greek term means to "cement together, to stick like glue, or to be welded together so the two cannot be separated without serious damage to both."

If you were to look at most failed marriages, you will find a failure to obey this very admonition to leave and cleave. Now the Bible has much more to say about marriage, but if we would just begin *here*—with this deceptively simple principle—we would be off to a strong, healthy start in our lifelong relationship.

WHEN IS DIVORCE PERMISSIBLE?

For the last few pages, I've shown you reasons to avoid divorce at all costs, and even how to keep yourself from the edge of the cliff. But is divorce ever permissible? Does the Bible allow for it at all?

The church seems to line up in two camps on this subject. Some say, "Divorce is *never* acceptable or permitted by God. If it is done, that person (who is divorced) can never remarry no matter what the cause, and is unsuitable for service to the Lord."

Others take a lax attitude, feeling "incompatibility" or "irreconcilable differences" are reasons enough to try again! I believe the answer lies somewhere between those two extremes. At the time of Christ, this lax attitude—taught by the Pharisees—was the prevailing opinion.

Here is what Jesus had to say about that topic, in very specific terms:

The Pharisees also came to Him, testing Him, and saying to Him, "Is it lawful for a man to divorce his wife for just any reason?"

And He answered and said to them, "Have you not read that He who made them at the beginning 'made them male and female,' and said, 'For this reason a man shall leave his father and mother and be joined to his wife, and the two shall become one flesh'? So then, they are no longer two but one flesh. Therefore what God has joined together, let not man separate."

They said to Him, "Why then did Moses command to give a certificate of divorce, and to put her away?"

He said to them, "Moses, because of the hardness of your hearts, permitted you to divorce your wives, but from the beginning it was not so. And I say to you, whoever divorces his wife, except for sexual immorality, and marries another, commits adultery; and whoever marries her who is divorced commits adultery."
(Matthew 19:3–9)

In this exchange, the Pharisees were preoccupied with the grounds for divorce…and Jesus with the institution of marriage. In Jesus' day the view of divorce was extremely liberal, and the practice was widespread in Israel. Consider the woman at the well, who had been married to five husbands.

Leading rabbis taught that a man could send away his wife for the most trivial of reasons. What it really boiled down to was *any reason*. As a result, people went into marriage in a half-hearted way, or were ready to "throw in the towel" at the first sign of trouble or conflict.

For this reason the Pharisees, energized by their usual motive of tripping up Jesus in any way they could, asked Him, "Why then, did Moses command that a man give his wife a certificate of divorce and send her away?" Jesus replied, "Moses permitted you to divorce your wives because your hearts were hard."

They said "commanded."

Jesus said "permitted."

Moses was authorized to do this because of the "callousness" or hardness of their hearts. This was with the idea of protecting the woman from the hardship of endeavoring to carry on in a home where she was unloved and unwanted, because the man had failed to realize the high ideal of marriage. Before the Mosaic Law came along, a man could simply say he no longer wanted his wife and turn her out of his house. As a result, she was totally vulnerable, and might be charged with adultery or unfaithfulness and be put to death! In order, then, to protect such a woman, this "bill of divorce" was allowed.

In this face-off with the cynical Pharisees, Jesus gives the number one reason for permitting divorce. In Matthew 19:9, He says, "I tell you that anyone who divorces his wife, except for sexual immorality, and marries another, commits adultery."

The term "sexual immorality" is from the Greek word *porneia*, meaning extramarital sexual relations. This also includes incest, prostitution, and homosexuality. Why? Because the oneness of the marriage bond has been violated. Paul wrote to the Corinthians that when a man had relations with a prostitute, he became "one with her."

This is not to say divorce because of adultery is mandatory—or even recommended. Every effort should be made to restore marriage, examining the steps that led to this tragic sin, and applying preventive measures to keep it from ever happening again. What God once glued together, He can mend and glue again.

Immorality, then, is not only grounds for divorce, it is also grounds for forgiveness!

Let me share the story of a woman named Dottie, told in her own words: "George had an affair when he was in his early forties. We went through hell for three years. I don't think the affair lasted that long, but the hell did. But when we came out of that crisis, we were one. It was so wonderful. George said, 'If it got any better, we just couldn't stand it.'

"Adultery is from the pit of hell, it destroys faith in the partner, security, love. But if we allow Him, God can take the ashes and bring such beautiful glory out of it, no one would believe it. Scripture says God can give 'beauty for ashes, joy instead of mourning, praise instead of despair.'"

There is one other reason given in Scripture where God will permit a divorce. In 1 Corinthians 7:13, Paul writes: "If a woman has a husband who is not a believer and he is willing to live with her, she must not divorce him [and vice versa]…. But if the unbeliever leaves, let him do so. A believing man or woman is not bound in such circumstances; God has called us to live in peace" (1 Corinthians 7:13, 15, NIV).

The term "not bound," or "bondage" used in this verse means "to be a slave, or held by consent of agreement."

And that's what sometimes happens. The unbelieving spouse simply deserts or leaves the other. If one marriage partner has made every effort to save the marriage, but the deserting partner simply refuses to stay, then the believer is free to dissolve the relationship, and remarry.

This does happen, and thank God He has provided a way of escape when a situation gets to this point. But again, as I have said, these situations are rare. Most marriages fall apart because people simply ignore what the Bible says, and go into the relationship in search of what the other person can do for them. When the predictable challenges of marriage kick in, they bail.

We cannot let that happen to us.

We can't let the flames of that destructive fire consume our home.

FIREPROOFING YOUR HOME

Remember the man whose house survived the

wildfire? When the smoke cleared, only his house, out of all the houses in that neighborhood, was left standing.

And why?

Because he was wise about the danger of fire in that part of the world, and he took the effort and trouble to make sure he was ready if the fire came. He said, "We went beyond what was required, and made it even safer."

That process can also include getting rid of dead trees, piled up brush, and long, dry grass around the immediate perimeter of the home. In other words, denying the wildfire handy fuel to race toward your home even faster.

I'm a married man, too, and I love my wife and my family more than I love my own life. But it's always dangerous to tell ourselves, "That happens to other people, but it could never happen to me. The fire might torch others' homes, but it won't burn mine."

That is a very dangerous attitude! Many other people whose marriages and families now lie in smoking ruin would have said the same thing before the flames consumed their house.

With that in mind, I must periodically step

back and ask myself some hard questions before the Lord. In a sense, I must check for "flammable materials" around my home that might add fuel to a fire I can't even see yet. Is there any relationship or pursuit I'm currently involved in that would put distance between me and my mate? Will this activity I've become involved in draw us together or drive us apart? Will it build our relationship up or tear it down? If you are a married person, you must ask yourself, "Are my mate and I leaving and cleaving? Are we in or out of God's order for our lives and marriage?"

When you think about it, life is awfully short.

It's here and then—before you can turn around two or three times—it's gone. Someday you're going to be in that rocker on the front porch, or in a retirement home sitting on a tiny little balcony in a lawn chair, or maybe lying on your death bed. And when you look back across your life, your career and your income level and all your accomplishments aren't going to mean very much.

But if, by the grace of God and through His enabling, your marriage stands strong through the flames, until death takes one of you home…If you can say, "Well, life wasn't perfect, but we walked through it together, and stayed faithful. We lived by those vows we made on our wedding day…'For richer or for poorer, in sickness and in health, to love and to cherish, till death do us part….'" If you can say that, no matter what else has happened to you through the ups and downs of your years, you'll find a smile crossing your face, and a peace that settles over your heart.

That's what I want. How about you?

10.

Four Words that Can
Change Your
Marriage

I f you were to drop in on our planet as an alien,
wander around a bit, and just study our Western
culture for a year or two, you'd probably return to
Planet X with at least a few firm conclusions.

As you wrote up your report for the Planetary
Exploration Society, you'd most likely say
something like, "Well, the people on earth that I
observed eat a lot of something they call 'fast food,'
spend a good deal of their time sitting in front of
a luminous screen they call 'TV,' keep a bunch
of domesticated animals called 'dogs' and 'cats'
around them, and finally, they seem to be experts
about 'love.' They must be experts, because the
word appears in so many of their songs and stories."

Aliens aside, it's true that you and I have heard
countless songs about love in our lives—ranging

from "All You Need Is Love" by the Beatles (who broke up not long after recording it), to that profound and insightful song "Yummy, Yummy, Yummy, I've Got Love in My Tummy" by a forgettable band called the Ohio Express.

We hear about people "making love," a phrase that used to mean romance and courting, but has morphed into a synonym for sex.

So, what exactly is love?

The dictionary defines it as "A profoundly tender, passionate affection, a feeling of warm personal attachment. Sexual desire or its gratification."

Is that it? Does that nail it? Is that what real love is? The kind of love that will last a lifetime? The kind of love that God commands us to have?

Absolutely not.

What a weak, wimpy definition.

Will "passionate affection" and "personal attachment" equip a marriage to ride the stormy waves of life and sustain it through darkness and trials, pressures and heartaches? Most people have "affection" and "attachment" to their dog! Is that God's standard for the union of a man and woman?

Not a chance. On the contrary, real love is

a radical, life-changing, lifelong pursuit. It is
a commitment as strong or stronger than the
commitment to life itself. People who have truly
understood the concept have literally laid down
their lives, sacrificing everything, for the one they
love.

Jesus Himself said, "Greater love has no one
than this, than to lay down one's life for his friends"
(John 15:13).

LEARNING TO LOVE

We must "learn to love." In fact, love must be
learned again and again. There is no end to it.
Hate, on the other hand, needs no instruction, but
waits only to be provoked. And apathy? Well you
don't need to do a thing to find that.

Learning to love is a lifelong occupation. A
full-time career. And it doesn't happen overnight.
Certainly there is that initial attraction that one
may have for a man or woman. It's pleasant, it's
exciting, it can be disorienting, and it can seize the
imagination like nothing else.

But it doesn't last forever.

One of the classic love stories of the Bible is
that of Jacob and Rachel. Jacob, son of Isaac, and

grandson of Abraham, had stolen the blessing
from his brother Esau, and was told by his mother
Rebecca to take a long vacation at her family's
sheep ranch hundreds of miles away—at least until
Esau cooled off.

After Jacob's long journey, he laid eyes for the
first time on the beautiful Rachel. He was smitten!
All the old clichés applied to him in that moment.
He fell. He flipped. He was lightning struck. He
went head-over-heels. He lost his heart.

Do you remember when you "fell in love" for
the first time? It may have been that boy or girl in
your grade school class. (If you were like me, the
objects of your crush never even knew you existed!)
Do you remember when you first laid eyes on the
person who was to be your spouse? Was it "love at
first sight"?

It certainly looks like that might have been the
case with Jacob. But really...what's so remarkable
about that? He had just walked off the backside
of the desert and the first thing he saw was a
stunningly beautiful woman. Being a red-blooded
Hebrew male, he noticed her. I mean really noticed
her. But when you think about it, Jacob didn't know
Rachel from Eve. He didn't know a thing about

her. At that point, all he knew was that "Rachel was beautiful in every way, with a lovely face and shapely figure" (Genesis 29:17, NLT). Now that physical attraction may be normal and nice, but again, it's not so remarkable.

I'll tell you what's remarkable: It's when two people have been looking at each other for year after year and love each other more than ever. *That* is remarkable. It's when a man and woman stay loyal and steadfast and loving through the long years and all the peaks and valleys of life. *That* is worth talking about.

LETTING LOVE MATURE

Maybe when you first saw your future spouse, it was all you could think about. You lost your appetite, had butterflies in your stomach, and your mouth went dry. You found yourself "tongue-tied." You literally thought about her (him) all day long.

That's great, but…would you really want to feel that way the rest of your life if you married that person? Can you imagine what that would be like? After twenty years of marriage you see your one-and-only at the breakfast table in her bathrobe, and say, "Uh, good morning honey! I don't have an appetite because I've been thinking about you all night. Wow, my heart sure is beating fast!"

That sounds more like a recipe for a heart attack than a lasting marriage! You need to mature in your love. That doesn't mean your love has gone somewhere, it simply means it's putting down roots and growing. It's coming out of the idealistic fantasy world and into the ebb and flow of real life.

Remember the first time you rode a bike or drove a car? Can you recall the exhilaration? The sheer excitement? It's not realistic to expect that same rush now, after driving for thirty years. Do you really want to salivate and have your heart race every time you get behind the wheel to drive to work in the morning? In the same way, it isn't realistic—or even desirable—to experience that initial "falling in love" phenomenon every day.

Speaking of "real love," C. S. Lewis wrote: "It is not merely a feeling, it is a deep unity, maintained by the will and deliberately strengthened by habit; reinforced by the grace which both parents ask, and receive from God. They can have this love for each other even at those moments when they do not like each other; as you love yourself even when you do not like yourself. They can retain this love even when each would easily, if they allowed themselves, be 'in love' with someone else. Being in love first moved them to promise fidelity: This quieter love enables them to keep the promise. It is on this love that engine of marriage is run. Being in love was the explosion that started it."

Jacob certainly experienced that explosion. Within a few weeks, he was proposing marriage. Rachel, however, had a conniving father named Laban who wanted to get some free work out of Jacob. So he struck a deal with his future son-in-law. "You work for me for seven years, and she's yours to marry!"

Then the long awaited wedding night came, they had a great feast, and old Laban pulled a fast one on Jacob. He slipped in his more plain daughter, Leah, in the place of Rachel for that "honeymoon night." Apparently, Leah and Rachel were somewhat alike. Perhaps Leah went along with this little masquerade thinking it was the only way she would ever get a husband. Whatever the case, Jacob was not a "happy camper" when he woke up and found Leah in his bed instead of his beloved Rachel! But to show his deep love for Rachel, he agreed to serve on the sheep ranch of

Laban & Sons for another seven years.

Now *that's* love. Most of us would have said to Laban, "I'm outta here! There are other fish in the sea, buddy!" But there in Genesis we're told why Jacob hung in there for his dear Rachel: *"So Jacob served seven years for Rachel, and they seemed only a few days to him because of the love he had for her"* (Genesis 29:20).

So Jacob's love was more than just the initial fireworks and heart palpitations. It was the real deal. The Bible says, "Many waters cannot quench love, neither can floods drown it" (Song of Solomon 8:7). This is the kind of love we need in our marriages today. And men, this is the kind of love God wants you to have for your wives.

Let me now identify for you *four words that can change your marriage*. They're found in the fifth chapter of Ephesians (and you've probably already figured out what they are).

"HUSBANDS, LOVE YOUR WIVES…"

And how are we supposed to do that? The rest of the passage answers that question.

> …just as Christ also loved the church and gave Himself for her, that He might sanctify

and cleanse her with the washing of water by the word, that He might present her to Himself a glorious church, not having spot or wrinkle or any such thing, but that she should be holy and without blemish. So husbands ought to love their own wives as their own bodies; he who loves his wife loves himself. For no one ever hated his own flesh, but nourishes and cherishes it, just as the Lord does the church. For we are members of His body, of His flesh and of His bones. "For this reason a man shall leave his father and mother and be joined to his wife, and the two shall become one flesh." This is a great mystery, but I speak concerning Christ and the church. Nevertheless let each one of you in particular so love his own wife as himself, and let the wife see that she respects her husband. (Ephesians 5:25–33)

Three times in eight verses men are told to simply "love your wives." And to do so as Christ loved the church! That's a tall order. That's setting the bar awfully high. Yes it is. But the fact of the matter is many marriages—including Christian marriages—are in trouble because men are unwilling to obey God's specific commands to them.

I heard the story of a woman and her husband who were heading toward a divorce. They felt their marriage was over, and wanted the pastor to simply acknowledge that. But the man of God was troubled, because he could see no biblical grounds for terminating the marriage. So the pastor said to the husband, "The Bible says you are to love your wife as Jesus Christ loved the church."

The husband replied, "Oh, I can't do that."

"Well," the pastor said, "if you can't begin at that level, then begin on a lower level. The Bible says you are to love your neighbor as yourself. Can you at least love her as a neighbor?"

"No," the man responded. "That's still too high a level."

To that the pastor replied, "Jesus also says to love your enemies. Begin *there*."

If you're a husband, there's no getting off the hook. You start where you are, and with God's help, you begin to love even beyond your capacity to love.

REVOLUTIONARY LOVE

Many women today don't realize how revolutionary a concept this "love your wives" command was in Paul's day. As I mentioned in the previous chapter, divorce was widespread in Israel at this time. False, unbiblical views of marriage and divorce had permeated the fabric of Judaism.

Amazingly, the pagan Greek world was even worse! There was no legal procedure for divorce in Greek society, since wives were simply the ones who cleaned the house and bore legitimate children. Men found their sexual enjoyment outside of marriage, so they didn't even bother to divorce their wives. The Athenian orator Demosthenes said, "We have courtesans for the sake of pleasure, we have concubines for the sake of daily cohabitation, and we have wives for the purpose of having children legitimately, and being faithful guardians for our household affairs."

Roman culture was no better. In fact, it treated the woman and wife as nothing more than a man's possession, to be discarded at will. So when Paul wrote these words under the inspiration of the Holy Spirit, it was revolutionary!

It sliced through the rotten fabric of

contemporary culture like a razor-sharp knife.

The wife is *not* some object or slave or item of property, she is "bone of your bones and flesh of your flesh" and you are to love her and *only* her!

So let's dispense with any revisionist history implying the Bible encourages the mistreatment of women. Absurd! In reality, it's the very opposite. *Husbands, love your wives!*

IT'S MORE THAN WORDS

Sadly, we *say* we "love our wives," but you wouldn't know it by the way we treat them. This kindness can often change with the passing of time. Some years ago the *Saturday Evening Post* ran an article entitled: "The Seven Stages of the Married Cold."

The first year: "Sugar dumpling, I'm really worried about my baby girl. You've got a bad sniffle and there's no telling about these things with all this strep going around. I'm putting you in the hospital this afternoon for a general checkup and a good rest. I know the food's lousy, but I'll be bringing your meals in from that gourmet restaurant you like so much."

The second year: "Listen darling, I don't like the sound of that cough. I've called the doctor and asked him to rush over here. Now you go to bed like a good girl, please, just for your loving husband, okay?"

The third year: "Maybe you'd better lie down, honey, nothing like a little rest when you feel lousy. I'll bring you something. Do we have any canned soup?"

The fourth year: "Now look, honey, be sensible. After you've fed the kids, washed the dishes, and finished the floors, you'd better lie down."

The fifth year: "Why don't you take a couple of Tylenol?"

The sixth year: "I wish you would just gargle or something instead of sitting around all evening barking like a seal."

The seventh year: "For Pete's sake, stop sneezing! Are you trying to give me pneumonia?"

In our English language we have basically only one word for love. It ranges from "I love my dog" to "I love my wife." We mean different things when we use that word.

The Greeks, however, had three different words for love. There was *eros,* which is love on a physical plane; *phileo,* love on an emotional plane; and, *agape,* love on a spiritual plane.

FIREWORKS AND FRIENDSHIP

Each of these "loves" has an important part to play in marriage. *Eros* encompasses that initial love, the mutual, physical attraction that draws a man and woman together. And we can celebrate that attraction, or the human race might die out in a generation or two! Sexual love plays a crucial role in marriage. The intimacy, closeness, and unmatched expression of oneness that married sex provides has a place that's just as important as being fruitful and producing children.

In the times in which we live, with so much of God's good plan warped and distorted, it's easy to forget that sex is a *God-given* desire. He wants us to enjoy what He has created to the full...but only within the protective bounds of marriage.

The book of Proverbs tells us,

Drink water from your own cistern,
And running water from your own well.
Should your fountains be dispersed abroad,
Streams of water in the streets?
Let them be only your own,
And not for strangers with you.
Let your fountain be blessed,
And rejoice with the wife of your youth.

As a loving deer and a graceful doe,
Let her breasts satisfy you at all times;
And always be enraptured with her love.
(Proverbs 5:15–19)

Do you see that word *enraptured*?

It means you need to get a little carried away. Other versions translate the same word *captivated, exhilarated, ravished, infatuated, filled with delight*. The root of the original word includes the imagery of "reeling, as though intoxicated."

There's a reason for that.

When Paul wrote to the church in Corinth, he was talking to a people surrounded by flagrant, in-your-face sexual immorality. Prostitutes were as common as coffee shops in Seattle. In this out-of-control sensual environment, it was more important than ever that husbands and wives were lovingly meeting each other's sexual needs. The apostle wrote: "But since there is so much immorality, each man should have his own wife, and each woman her own husband" (1 Corinthians 7:2, NIV).

Paul elaborated further, saying, "The husband should fulfill his marital duty to his wife and likewise the wife to her husband. The wife's body does not belong to her alone but also to her husband. In the same way the husband's body does not belong to him alone but to his wife. Do not deprive each other except by mutual consent and for a time, so that you may devote yourselves to prayer. Then come together again so that Satan will not tempt you because of your lack of self-control" (vv. 3–5).

To fail to meet this need in your mate's life leaves him or her more open to sexual temptation.

So *eros* is good…as far as it goes.

The problem with *eros*, however, is that it is essentially selfish. It is primarily interested in *taking*. It says, "I have needs, and I want them met." That isn't bad, but it's not what you build an entire marriage on.

In contrast, *phileo* takes, but also desires to give. It's friendship love, companionship love, like the type that Jesus and Peter shared. It is love that comes as a result of a pleasure or delight one draws from the object loved.

THE BEST LOVE OF ALL

The third love mentioned in Scripture, *agape*, springs from a sense of the preciousness of the object rather than the sense of pleasure derived.

Agape is primarily determined by the character of the one who loves—not necessarily the "lovableness" of the object. *Agape* is not a feeling or emotion. It gives, wanting nothing in return.

And guess what? This is the kind of love God is speaking of when He commands us as husbands to love our wives. "Husbands, *agape* your wives...."

Love as the world describes it is always object-oriented. A person is loved because of physical attractiveness, personality, wit, prestige, or some feature or trait that we find appealing.

People magazine has an issue where it names "The World's Most Beautiful People." I've never seen an issue where they feature "The World's Most Ordinary People." I don't think so. No one would buy it. We value and worship beauty and talent.

In his excellent book *Love Life for Every Married Couple*, Dr. Ed Wheat writes: "Even in the best of marriages, unlovable traits show up in both partners, and in *every* marriage, sooner or later, a need arises that can be met only by unconditional love! *Agape* is the kind of love we need in these situations. This love has the capacity to persist in the face of rejection and continue where there is no human response at all. It can leap over walls that would stop any human love cold. It is never deflected by unlovable behavior and gives gladly to the undeserving without totaling the cost. To the relationship of husband and wife, which would otherwise lie at the mercy of fluctuating emotions and human upheavals, *agape* imparts stability and a permanence that is rooted in the eternal. *Agape* is the divine solution for marriages populated by imperfect human beings!"

LOVE THROUGH A PRISM

The Bible gives us the definitive illustration of this highest form of love in 1 Corinthians 13. The apostle writes:

> Love suffers long and is kind, love does not envy, love does not parade itself, is not puffed up, does not behave rudely, does not seek its own, is not provoked, thinks no evil, does not rejoice in iniquity, but rejoices in the truth; bears all things, believes all things, hopes all things, endures all things. (verses 4–6)

In this well-known passage of Scripture, Paul

holds up a prism to the brilliance of *agape* love,
and—from just these two verses—we see it shine
out in fifteen beautiful colors and hues, each ray
showing a different facet. These verses do not focus
so much on what love is, as much as they focus on
what love does or does not do.

Agape love is active, not abstract or passive.
It doesn't simply "feel patient," it *is* patient.
It practices patience. It doesn't just have kind
feelings, it does kind things. *Agape* love means
action, not just a benign attitude. *Agape* love
means involvement, not just a comfortable
detachment from the needs of others. *Agape* love
means unconditionally loving the unlovable, the
undeserving, and the unresponsive. *Agape* love
means we can love our mates even in the face of
extremely unlovely and unlovable behavior.

Love is fully love only when it *acts*. The apostle
John wrote: "My little children, let us not love in
word or in tongue, but in deed and in truth"
(1 John 3:18). The purpose of Paul's prism is not to
give a "technical analysis" of love, but to break it
down into "bite size" pieces so we may more easily
understand it and apply it in a practical way.

If you want to see how far you have to go to

reach the level of this mountain-peak standard, just try inserting your name wherever you find the word "love" in this chapter.

But the truth is, there is only one name that fits as a perfect substitute for "love" in 1 Corinthians 13, and that name is Jesus. In essence, this chapter is a portrait of Jesus.

Let's look a little closer at some of the specifics.

Agape love is patient.

The word used here literally means "long tempered." It's a common term in the New Testament, and is used almost exclusively of being patient with people, rather than circumstances or events. Love's patience is the ability to be inconvenienced or taken advantage of by a person over and over again. This is the love Jesus spoke of that "turns the other cheek." Its primary concern is for the welfare of others, not itself.

Agape love is kind.

Just as patience will take anything from others, kindness will give anything to others. God is our supreme model in this. The Bible says, "Do you think lightly of the riches of His kindness and forbearance and patience? Not knowing that the kindness [goodness] of God leads you to repentance?" (cf. Romans 2:4). As we model the love of Christ, His goodness, to our wife, she will in almost all cases respond by "submitting unto us as unto the Lord." And why is that? Because we are *behaving* like the Lord! And why does the church submit to Jesus Christ? Because of His unconditional *agape* love for us, that won us over. "We love Him because He first loved us."

PRACTICAL KINDNESS

Yes, the *agape* love a husband is to have for his wife is kind. This love shows itself practically: Tenderness, gifts, a listening, sympathetic ear, simple courtesy, and telling her you love her. In Proverbs 31, we read of a woman whose "children call her blessed and her husband praises her."

When was the last time you "praised your wife" in front of the kids, friends, or even strangers? This is hard for many men. It's not that they don't love their wives; in fact, some of these husbands love their wives so deeply they would lay down their very lives for them. These same guys might look at their wives and in a quiet moment think to themselves, *You know, I really love this woman*. It's just that verbal communication doesn't always come as easily to a man.

He thinks it. He feels it. But he has difficulty saying it.

Consider this: A woman speaks an average of 50,000 words a day. In the same amount of time, a man speaks only 25,000 (and he uses up 24,840 at work). That leaves about 160 for his wife every evening…so he'd better make them count! The truth is, even when words are lacking, a hug and a kiss can go a long way! A kiss is a wonderful way to show your love—and it turns out, it may even add years to your life.

A German group of psychologists, physicians, and insurance companies cooperated on a research project designed to find the secret to long life and success. In the process, they made a surprising discovery.

The secret? "Kiss your wife each morning when you leave for work!" The meticulous German researchers discovered that men who kiss their wives every morning have fewer automobile accidents on their way to work than men who omit the morning kiss. The good-morning kissers miss less work because of sickness, and earn 20 to 30 percent more money than non-kissers.

A hug would even be nice. I read about a couple that was having some marital trouble, so they went to see their pastor. After a few visits, and a lot of questioning and listening, the pastor said that he had discovered the main problem. He stood up, went over to the woman, asked her to stand, and gave her a hug. He looked at the man and said, "This is what your wife needs, at least once a day!"

The man frowned, thought for a moment, then said, "Okay, what time do you want me to bring her back tomorrow?"

In this same portion of Scripture, Paul also gives us eight negative descriptions.

WHAT LOVE IS NOT

Agape love does not envy. Trust is an essential ingredient to any successful marriage. Jealousy, though clothed in the guise of love, is in reality a destructive sin. James writes: "But if you harbor bitter envy and selfish ambition in your hearts, do not boast about it or deny the truth. Such 'wisdom' does not come down from heaven but is earthly, unspiritual, of the devil. For where you have envy and selfish ambition, there you find disorder and every evil practice" (James 3:14–16).

Agape love does not "parade itself." In other words, it doesn't boast about its accomplishments. Bragging is the other side of jealousy. Jealousy is wanting what someone else has; bragging is trying to make others jealous of what we have.

Love doesn't constantly remind your mate of the great "sacrifice" you've made for her.

Maybe you have! Good for you. But *agape* love doesn't strut it around, doesn't deliberately drop it into conversation to make an impression.

Agape love does not behave rudely. A rude person cares nothing about the feelings and sensitivities of others. Many husbands have more manners toward a complete stranger than the one who is "bone of their bones, flesh of their flesh."

Agape love is not provoked. This refers to those things which trigger a flash of anger within us, sometimes leading to an outburst. And if we are provoked now and then (and we will be), Ephesians 4:26 (NIV) has this command: "'In your anger do not sin': Do not let the sun go down while you are still angry." Don't ever give unconfessed sin a chance to send down its ugly roots! Leave it until morning to deal with and it will be much harder to uproot.

A husband and his wife decided to put

Ephesians 4:26 into practice: *"Do not let the sun go down while you are still angry."* So they made up their minds never to go to bed mad at each other.

Some thirty years later someone asked, "How did it work out?"

"Very well," replied the husband, "but sometimes it was a little rough sitting up all night."

WHO CAN LIVE LIKE THIS?

Agape love thinks no evil. The word *think* in this phrase is a bookkeeping term that means "to calculate, enter into a ledger, a permanent record that can be consulted when needed." In other words, love doesn't dredge up old arguments, incidents, or I-told-you-so's out of the past.

Agape love believes all things. It believes the best of every person. It's not suspicious or cynical. If a loved one is accused of something wrong, love will consider her (him) innocent until proven guilty!

Agape love endures all things. It refuses to give up, surrender, or stop believing or hoping. Love will simply not walk away—no matter what. Winston Churchill astutely observed, "Victory is not obtained through evacuation."

Sometimes when some friction arises in the marriage someone will say, "I'm leaving you!" Or, "I'm getting a hotel room," or "I want a separation." You'd better have an awfully good reason for a step like that. Genuine love, *agape* love, endures and hangs in there.

After reading this chapter, you might find yourself saying, "Greg, who can live like this? Who could ever love like this?"

No one can.

No one but Jesus.

And yet this is the standard to which He calls us. Listen, the only way to live a life of divine love is to have the Divine One living within you. Scripture tells us that "the love of God has been poured out in our hearts by the Holy Spirit who was given to us" (Romans 5:5).

Some might say, "Well, I'll just wait around until God lays it on me, until He gives me this special love." If you are a Christian, my friend, *He already has*. It's time by faith and obedience to begin demonstrating it! Don't wait for the right mood or feeling or inspiration. Just roll up your sleeves and begin to do it, live it, walk it, trusting God to supply what you don't (yet) possess. Loving feelings will often follow loving actions, but even if they don't, it is God's clear command for husbands to love their wives…and obedience always brings blessing.

May God help us as husbands to take that step of faith, and start applying those four words that can change and transform our marriages.

Conclusion

We have a God who wants us to live well, to succeed in our marriages, to enjoy our families, to understand His will and desire for our lives, and to escape the riptides and undertows that drag us down.

In an often quoted verse from the book of Jeremiah, the Lord says, "For I know the thoughts that I think toward you…thoughts of peace and not of evil, to give you a future and a hope" (29:11).

To His own people about to enter the Promised Land, God said, "Today I have given you the choice between life and death, between blessings and curses. I call on heaven and earth to witness the choice you make. Oh, that you would choose life, that you and your descendants might live!" (Deuteronomy 30:19, NLT).

Jesus said, "My purpose is to give life in all its fullness" (John 10:10, NLT).

There's no doubt about it, the world we live in can seem hard and unjust and painful at times. But at the core of it all, we have a God who is *for* us. From His wide-angle perspective on high, He can help us to avoid the traps, the pitfalls, the mistakes, and the failures that mar our lives and darken our days.

That's the reason for this book. These "top ten" messages selected by my radio audience are all about finding the best path through this sometimes difficult terrain we call life. We've wrestled with some big questions, we've zeroed in on some surprising aspects about the battle between good and evil, we've taken a closer look at God's plan for a successful, happy marriage…and we've learned what it really means to experience forgiveness of our sins and grasp the eternal life freely available to us in relationship with Jesus Christ.

Life *can* be better. Right here in our everyday lives on earth, and on into that endless day when we walk through heaven's gate and into His presence.

That is what God wants for your life.

And what God wants, God knows how to deliver.

About the Author

Greg Laurie is the pastor of Harvest Christian Fellowship (one of America's largest churches) in Riverside, California. He is the author of over thirty books, including the Gold Medallion Award winner *The Upside-Down Church.* You can find his study notes in the *New Believer's Bible* and the *Seeker's Bible.* Host of the *Harvest: Greg Laurie* television program and the nationally syndicated radio program, *A New Beginning,* Greg Laurie is also the founder and featured speaker for Harvest Crusades—contemporary, large-scale evangelistic outreaches, which local churches organize nationally and internationally. He serves on the board of directors of the Billy Graham Evangelistic Association and Samaritan's Purse. He and his wife, Cathe, have two children and live in Southern California.

STEPS TO PEACE WITH GOD

1. RECOGNIZE GOD'S PLAN—PEACE AND LIFE

The message you have read in this book stresses that God loves you and wants you to experience His peace and life.

The BIBLE says ... For God loved the world so much that He gave His only Son, so that everyone who believes in Him may not die but have eternal life. John 3:16

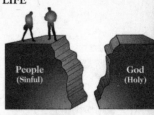

2. REALIZE OUR PROBLEM—SEPARATION FROM GOD

People choose to disobey God and go their own way. This results in separation from God.

The BIBLE says ... Everyone has sinned and is far away from God's saving presence. Romans 3:23

3. RESPOND TO GOD'S REMEDY—CROSS OF CHRIST

God sent His Son to bridge the gap. Christ did this by paying the penalty of our sins when He died on the cross and rose from the grave.

The BIBLE says ... But God has shown us how much He loves us—it was while we were still sinners that Christ died for us! Romans 5:8

4. RECEIVE GOD'S SON—LORD AND SAVIOR

You cross the bridge into God's family when you ask Christ to come into your life.

The BIBLE says ... Some, however, did receive Him and believed in Him; so He gave them the right to become God's children. John 1:12

THE INVITATION IS TO:
REPENT (turn from your sins), ASK for God's forgiveness, and by faith RECEIVE Jesus Christ into your heart and life and follow Him in obedience as your Lord and Savior.

PRAYER OF COMMITMENT
"Dear Lord Jesus, I know that I am a sinner, and I ask for Your forgiveness. I believe You died for my sins and rose from the dead. I turn from my sins and invite You to come into my heart and life. I want to trust and follow You as my Lord and Savior. In Your Name, Amen."

If you are committing your life to Christ, please let us know!

Billy Graham Evangelistic Association
1 Billy Graham Parkway, Charlotte, NC 28201-0001
1-877-2GRAHAM (1-877-247-2426)
billygraham.org